Soul Care
Quick Reference

SOUL CARE
QUICK REFERENCE

THOMAS NELSON BIBLES
A Division of Thomas Nelson, Inc.
www.ThomasNelson.com

Produced with the assistance of the Livingstone
Corporation. Project Staff include: Katie E. Gieser,
Christopher D. Hudson, Mary Larsen, Jackie Sager, and
Linda Taylor.

Printed in the United States of America
1 2 3 4 5 6 7—06 05 04 03 02 01

Table of Contents

Abortion

Psalm 139:16

Your eyes saw my substance, being yet unformed. And in Your book they all were written, the days fashioned for me, when as yet there were none of them.

 The abortion debate focuses on the unborn babies who have died, the people who are responsible for those deaths, and those who are standing for God's truth. The abortion issue is not only about death; it is about life and God Himself, the Creator of life. The sanctity of life is a biblical principle. God purposefully brings people into this world in order that He might have a personal relationship with them. The Bible tells us that God knew us even before we were born.

Christians must communicate the sanctity of life by speaking the truth in love (Eph. 4:15). Abortion is a corrupt practice and Christians must communicate this truth gently and confidently. Our goal should be to educate people, to help them understand the truth about abortion, and ultimately to draw them to Christ and His salvation. Many people who have previously been involved in giving abortions have been transformed through the power of Jesus Christ. Many who have had abortions—and have been devastated by them—have experienced Jesus' healing touch. It is important for Christians to confidently stand up for unborn children, for that means that they are standing up for life and for truth.

For more on abortion, see the article by Craig and Janet Parshall in **The Soul Care Bible**, page 786 (Ps. 139:16).

Abuse

Judges 19:25

But the men would not heed him. So the man took his concubine and brought her out to them. And they knew her and abused her all night until morning; and when the day began to break, they let her go.

These verses leave us with no doubt that horrible abuse has occurred for thousands of years. It is a fact that many people, especially children, are abused every year. The Church must assume that even among its own members are some who are suffering from present abuse or bear the scars of past abuse. Believers need to willingly help these hurting people. As we become aware of their pain, we need to be willing to reach out in comfort and love.

There is hope for the abused person. God's great power can heal the deepest scars. He can be trusted to replace pain and hurt with His comfort and love. But it will take time. Focusing on God's power is an emotional stepladder toward healing. People will need to face their wounds and understand their root causes. They will need to answer questions about how they were hurt and who hurt them. They will need to answer the tough questions, face some difficult facts, deal with anger that has perhaps been buried, and then learn how to move on. God's promises in His Word will help them. God's love will draw them close. True healing will come from God alone—He knows and understands.

For more on abuse, see the article by Diane Langberg in **The Soul Care Bible**, page 328 (Judg. 19:25).

Accountability

Jeremiah 3:11

Then the LORD said to me, "Backsliding Israel has shown herself more righteous than treacherous Judah."

Just as Israel and Judah were accountable to God for their actions, so every believer is accountable to God. When Christians pray and ask God to show them areas where help is needed in their lives, God will reveal their weaknesses to them. Many times God will use other people. This is where accountability should take place. Accountability involves a relationship where people hold each other accountable for their thoughts and actions, seeking to obey God, improve in a certain area, or stay away from sin. This is done by openly discussing those thoughts and actions, holding them up against the standard of God's Word, and then evaluating how to improve. Accountability requires openness and honesty. If denial, lies, blame, or pride get in the way of accountability, it loses its purpose.

There are four types of accountability. *Restorative accountability* restores others to a relationship or to a church membership after they have sinned. *Preventative accountability* guards against temptation to sin. *Constructive accountability* encourages and develops spiritual growth. *Task-oriented accountability* holds others to keeping promises and meeting goals.

Believers need to share their burdens with one another and help one another. Accountability supports and encourages spiritual growth in the body of Christ.

For more on **accountability**, see the article by Jesse Dillinger in **The Soul Care Bible**, page 966 (Jer. 3:11).

13

Addictions

Habakkuk 2:5

"Indeed, because he transgresses by wine, he is a proud man, and he does not stay at home. Because he enlarges his desire as hell, and he is like death, and cannot be satisfied, he gathers to himself all nations and heaps up for himself all peoples."

Habakkuk understood the problems inherent with addiction to alcohol. Addiction occurs when the brain becomes dependent upon substances it produces when the addict engages in certain behaviors. Over time, more of the substance is needed to get the same effect. The substances to which these people are addicted become associated with the relief of certain emotions, certain "high" feelings, which makes breaking the addiction difficult. Not only do people become addicted to chemicals such as drugs and alcohol, but those who have sexual fantasies or who gamble also experience chemical production in their brains that makes these practices addicting.

Recovery from addiction requires work. Spiritually, addicts must confess their powerlessness. Emotionally, the addict must face old wounds. It is helpful to face these feelings in a group setting where there is accountability. Physically, medical intervention may be needed.

Addicts are typically lonely or angry. Many never learned how to form healthy attachments to others, so they try unsuccessfully to control their own lives without help from God or others. Their addictions eventually lead to destructive consequences. A hunger for God and for fellowship underlies all addictions. Helping addicts recover involves addressing these underlying needs.

For more on addictions, see the article by Mark R. Laaser in **The Soul Care Bible**, page 1186 (Hab. 2:5–7).

Adolescent Development

Daniel 1:8

But Daniel purposed in his heart that he would not defile himself with the portion of the king's delicacies, nor with the wine which he drank; therefore he requested of the chief of the eunuchs that he might not defile himself.

 Daniel was an adolescent of strong faith and character. The years of adolescence provide unique challenges. Fear, feelings, friends, and faith are four crucial areas during this time.

A huge part of navigating teenagers through adolescence is helping them understand what is happening to them in the various areas of their lives. The many social, physical, and emotional changes they experience can be frightening at times. We need to help them live above their fears. Loneliness, depression, anxiousness, and low self-worth are some of the feelings that face the typical teenager during this period where much of their identity is formed. It is important to teach adolescents how to "take captive" the thoughts and feelings that contradict God's Word (2 Cor. 10:5).

As adolescents are tempted to compromise their morals for the sake of acceptance, it is vital that we encourage them to "not be conformed to this world" (Rom. 12:2), but to be like Daniel and not give in to peer pressure (Dan. 1:8). Finally, adolescence is a period of great questioning and wrestling with faith issues. Rebellion is sometimes involved. Adults need to assure teenagers of God's unconditional love and acceptance without squelching this character-building process.

For more on **adolescent development**, see the article by Dawson McAllister in **The Soul Care Bible**, page 1104 (Dan. 1:8).

Adolescent Problems

2 Samuel 15:10

Then Absalom sent spies throughout all the tribes of Israel, saying, "As soon as you hear the sound of the trumpet, then you shall say, 'Absalom reigns in Hebron!'"

 David's son Absalom was rebelling—in many ways he was a typical teenager, except that his father was the king! Yet, like Absalom, teenagers today are also growing up in a prosperous society. They have outstanding opportunities, yet they feel disconnected, lacking a sense of personal identity.

When a child enters adolescence he or she may no longer be quick to obey and easy to control. Many parents respond to the change by laying down more rules, attempting to provide more structure. These rules often leave teens feeling even more disconnected from their families. Parents need to present rules in the context of loving relationships in order to gain a positive response to those rules. Teenagers need to know that they are more important to their parents than the rules. A relational context must be in place for the rules that govern a family. Relationship was important God. God always treated Israel with love, doing everything for their good, even though they were rebellious at times. The Law was God's way of protecting and providing for His people.

Not all children will rebel, but many will. Parents can survive turbulent times of adolescence with love, open communication, and constant prayer.

For more on **adolescent problems**, see the article by Josh McDowell in **The Soul Care Bible**, page 410 (2 Sam. 15).

Adultery

Hosea 1:2

When the LORD began to speak by Hosea, the LORD said to Hosea: "Go, take yourself a wife of harlotry and children of harlotry, for the land has committed great harlotry by departing from the LORD."

 God experienced the pain of adultery when His chosen people, Israel, betrayed Him by worshiping other gods. His prophet Hosea became a living example of that pain. Adultery is devastating, but healing is possible.

Many factors impact the rise of infidelity in marriages. Some people expect their spouses to meet emotional needs that were never met in their childhood. Spouses who experienced physical and sexual abuse, were exposed to pornography, and have a family history of alcoholism often fall into unfaithfulness. Avoidance of intimacy, conflict, or stress can cause a marriage to be vulnerable to infidelity.

Restoration of a marriage is possible because of the Holy Spirit's work in the healing process. Restoration involves work for both spouses. They must first understand the cause of the infidelity. Next, they can begin to rebuild trust by being honest with each other and by showing affection and affirmation in non-sexual ways. Finally, both spouses much take time for restoration and enrichment of the marriage.

Christians are called to be supportive friends to those recovering from adultery. We can pray for and listen to them. We must also spend more time and energy on our own marriages to make sure they are not vulnerable to infidelity.

For more on **adultery**, see the article by David M. Carder in **The Soul Care Bible**, page 1128 (Hos. 1).

Aging/Elderly

Joshua 14:10, 11

"And now, behold, the LORD has kept me alive, as He said, these forty-five years, ever since the LORD spoke this word to Moses while Israel wandered in the wilderness; and now, here I am this day, eighty-five years old. As yet I am as strong this day as on the day that Moses sent me; just as my strength was then, so now is my strength for war, both for going out and for coming in."

 Caleb was an old man, but he was by no means finished with what he wanted to do in life! Though western society glorifies youth, old age can be an enjoyable phase of life. It is a matter of attitude, determination, and hope. God encourages Christians through His Word to be satisfied, even excited, to reach the golden years.

As we live with our worldly concerns, we often forget that our ultimate home is in heaven. Our lives are merely a preliminary to an eternity with God. Our years on this earth, no matter how many or how few, are no more than a blink when compared with forever. When we understand this, we can focus our sights on heaven; as we get older, we should even anticipate and look forward to it. With our eyes directed upward, we can trust God to use our golden years for Him, even as our bodies show signs of slowing down. Every moment of our lives has been planned for us by God. As we live on into our later years, we can see what God would have us do for Him. And when He comes for us, we'll be ready!

For more on **aging/elderly**, see the article by David Seamands in **The Soul Care Bible**, page 282 (Josh. 14).

Anger

Psalm 19:14

Let the words of my mouth and the meditation of my heart be acceptable in Your sight, O LORD, my strength and my Redeemer.

 Anger is a strong feeling of displeasure or irritation. When we feel really angry, it's difficult for our words and our thoughts to be pleasing to God, as the psalmist desired. The emotion of anger sends energy into the nervous system and causes us to want to react. We don't have a choice about whether to feel angry, but we do have a choice about whether we will react in a constructive or destructive way.

Unhealthy anger occurs when people allow their anger to control them. They seek revenge and are likely to react in a destructive way. Healthy anger, on the other hand, is dependent on the help and guidance of the Holy Spirit. According to the Bible, we are to be angry without sinning (Eph. 4:26). People with healthy anger will use their emotional energy to confront evil, right wrongs, and change situations for the good.

There are steps we can take to confront and control unhealthy anger. When we are aware of our anger, accept responsibility, identify the source, and choose how to invest anger energy, we can stop destructive anger. The Holy Spirit and God's Word can help us replace the unhealthy emotional responses with healthy ones.

For more on anger, see the article by Gary J. Oliver in **The Soul Care Bible**, page 692 (Ps. 19:14).

Anxiety

Philippians 4:6

Be anxious for nothing, but in everything by prayer and supplication, with thanksgiving, let your requests be made known to God.

 Anxiety and worry have much to do with the pace at which people live, get in debt, and are disconnected from others. In our society today, there is an increased prevalence of anxiety disorders as a result of these factors.

It is important to recognize the differences between fear, worry, anxiety, and anxiety disorders. *Fear* is triggered when we feel threatened, whether it is in response to a real or perceived danger. It can also be felt when imagining undesired situations or outcomes. *Worry* is a mental exercise that tries to solve situations beyond our control. *Anxiety* is a pervasive, inner feeling of nervousness, unrest, and uneasiness that lasts for an extended period. *Anxiety* disorders are indicated by unexplained, frequent, and intense anxiety that can be either sudden, lasting several hours, or constant. Generalized anxiety, phobias, obsessive-compulsive disorder, post-traumatic stress disorder, and panic attacks are all types of anxiety disorders.

People with anxiety and anxiety disorders may require extra intervention in order to get the help they need. Such difficulties can and should be treated in order for the person to be able to carry on a full and anxiety-free life.

For more on anxiety, see the article by Archibald D. Hart in **The Soul Care Bible**, page 1568 (Phil. 4).

Attachment/Blessing

Genesis 49:28

And [Jacob] blessed them; he blessed each one according to his own blessing.

 In Old Testament times, a father would pass along a special blessing to his sons. The portion recorded in Genesis 49 gives Abraham's blessings to his twelve sons. The Hebrew word for *blessing*, however, is used throughout the Old Testament, picturing God's blessing upon all of his children. The example of God's blessing of his people provides a context for discussion of our providing a blessing to our children and to those who are in close relationships with us. People will flourish when they are blessed by those they love.

There are five basic elements to blessing others. These include: (1) *meaningful touch* that communicates warmth and acceptance, (2) a *spoken message* that includes words of affirmation and praise, (3) *attaching high value*, referring to words that communicate the person's value based simply on who he or she is, (4) *picturing a special future*, meaning encouraging a person regarding their gifts and character traits that God will use in the future, and (5) *active commitment to fulfill the blessing*, meaning a commitment to do everything possible to help the person be successful.

Acting on these five elements will bring warmth, healing, and hope to all of our intimate relationships.

For more on **attachment/blessing**, see the article by John Trent in **The Soul Care Bible**, page 76 (Gen. 49).

Attitudes

Micah 6:8

He has shown you, O man, what is good; and what does the LORD require of you but to do justly, to love mercy, and to walk humbly with your God?

God's peace cannot dwell in the hearts of Christians who live with negative attitudes. God gave us three requirements in Micah 6:8, which we must follow in order to live with positive attitudes.

The first requirement is to "do justly." We need to live honestly and face the problems of our hearts. Then we must confess to God what is in our hearts and minds. The second requirement is to "love mercy." We need to be merciful and forgiving toward others, working to have right relationships. The third requirement is to "walk humbly." By submitting our minds to Christ, we put Him and others ahead of ourselves. When we put others first, we can experience God's peace and joy and live with positive attitudes.

In order to develop and maintain positive attitudes, we must cultivate a spiritual life by daily spending time in God's Word and in prayer, giving our worries to God, and being obedient to Him. When we do this, we will experience the peace of God in our hearts. Although having a positive attitude does not free us from having difficulties in life, it gives us peace knowing that we can do anything through Christ.

For more on attitudes, see the article by Daniel Lovett in **The Soul Care Bible**, page 1174 (Mic. 6:8).

Belief

If you confess with your mouth the Lord Jesus and believe in your heart that God has raised Him from the dead, you will be saved. For with the heart one believes unto righteousness, and with the mouth confession is made unto salvation.

 God wants us to believe the truth so we can experience abundant life. Many times, faulty thinking creeps into our minds. This leads to emotional and spiritual problems. We need to renew our minds so that we may believe the truth and gain righteousness through salvation.

God is truth, but our enemy, Satan, is the father of lies (John 8:44). Satan wants us to not believe the truth, but instead to believe his lies—lies that he wants to use to destroy us. Satan's lies may sound like this: "I must be perfect," "I must have everyone's love and approval," "Things have to go my way for me to be happy," "Life should be easy," or "God hates the sin and the sinner." If we believe these lies, we cannot then believe God's truth. We become stunted spiritually, we cannot grow, and we will face problems from without and within. When we believe Satan's lies, we cannot help God's kingdom.

So the key to renewing our minds is to focus on God's truth. First, we must believe in the Lord Jesus Christ and be saved. Then we must read and believe the promises in His Word.

For more on belief, see the article by Chris Thurman in **The Soul Care Bible**, page 1480 (Rom. 10:9, 10).

Bitterness

Job 21:25

"Another man dies in the bitterness of his soul, never having eaten with pleasure."

 Job was a man who experienced excruciating suffering. God also understands suffering, for Jesus endured agonizing suffering when He died on the cross, took our sins upon Himself, and endured separation from God. God takes no joy in our pain. The Bible tells us that God uses suffering to draw us back to Him and to teach us patience and endurance. He allows suffering in our lives in order to accomplish His good plan. God wants us to learn to hate sin, to grow spiritually, and to love and trust Him completely.

Yet if we are not watchful, suffering can have the opposite effect. It can turn our focus away from God and onto ourselves. We can become bitter unless we learn to be content in spite of our suffering. Contentment comes when we pursue God. He will not fail us. Sometimes His answer to our pleas for healing or escape from pain is "no." He does not always allow us to escape suffering because He wants us to strengthen our commitment to Christ and depend on His grace. When we focus on God and overcome bitterness, our hope is stretched, our faith is increased, and our character is strengthened.

For more on **bitterness**, see the article by Joni Eareckson Tada in **The Soul Care Bible**, page 658 (Job 21:22–26).

Blended Families

Genesis 29:28

So [Laban] gave [Jacob] his daughter Rachel as wife also.

 The Bible describes some blended families that surely had great adjustments! The blended families we describe here, however, result because of remarriage. Everything old and familiar becomes strange and new, and parents need to be sensitive. The children in blended families face many adjustments: a new parent and perhaps new siblings, a change in living arrangements, which could lead to a change in schools, churches, and friendships. Blended families also face the challenge of working their different histories together— how to celebrate the holidays and birthdays, where to go on vacation, even daily routines. From the new parent and other family members, the children will experience different methods of discipline, and different expressions of affection, anger, and frustration. There will be relational struggles as the children adjust to this new arrangement. Visitation arrangements can also add a whole new level of stress.

Parents need to be very careful to help their children adjust. It will take some time, and both parents need to be sensitive. As you seek to build a strong marriage and continue to give both consistent love, affection, and guidance, you will help your children find the security they need.

For more on **blended families**, see the article by David R. Miller in **The Soul Care Bible**, page 46 (Gen. 29).

Boundaries

Exodus 20:1–3

And God spoke all these words, saying: "I am the LORD your God, who brought you out of the land of Egypt, out of the house of bondage. You shall have no other gods before Me."

 Some people complain that the Bible is nothing but a book of rules and regulations. In reality, the rules God gives are what really allows for freedom. The "rules" aren't really rules at all. They're boundaries. These Ten Commandments provide very important boundaries that form the basis for a safe society.

A boundary is a line drawn between what is yours and what is your neighbor's. When God sets boundaries, he is doing so for our own good. God uses boundaries so that Christians can be safe and happy with one another. Boundaries promote love, define what is our responsibility and what is not, and protect our freedom.

Boundaries not only help Christians understand their relationship with God, but they also define our relationships and responsibilities to one another. They prevent dangerous habits and lifestyles. Boundaries give us true freedom.

How do we set good boundaries? We need to read God's Word. From His Word we can discover where we should draw our personal boundary lines in all areas of our lives. When we have those lines in place and stand firm within them, then we are truly free.

For more on **boundaries**, see the article by Henry Cloud and John Townsend in **The Soul Care Bible**, page 106 (Ex. 20:1–17).

Burnout

Isaiah 40:31

But those who wait on the LORD shall renew their strength; they shall mount up with wings like eagles, they shall run and not be weary, they shall walk and not faint.

Everyone has stress, but when we exceed our physical limits, we become overloaded and face the possibility of burnout.

Jesus was able to prioritize His life and focus on the important things. We, on the other hand, are constantly in a hurry and are quick to say "yes" to everything. We need to learn from Jesus' example and wait on God. The Bible gives some practical ways of avoiding burnout.

We must never allow our schedules to be under the world's control, but always understand that our time is God's. We should acknowledge our limits and make sure that our schedules allow time for rest. We can consciously slow the pace of life by defining and defending our personal boundaries. Although He could have, Jesus did not heal every single person in Israel. We cannot expect to do more than He did.

We need to learn how to say "no," for that will keep us from overload. Then, we will have less things to do, but they will be the right things and we will be able to do them well. When we can do this, our strength will be renewed; we will "walk and not faint."

For more on **Burnout**, see the article by H. B. London in **The Soul Care Bible**, page 920 (Is. 40:31).

Change/Maturity

2 Corinthians 5:17

Therefore, if anyone is in Christ, he is a new creation; old things have passed away; behold, all things have become new.

 The Bible teaches that believers are "new creations." Part of being "new" means a deep desire to be more like Christ and to grow to maturity in our faith.

Maturity comes when we are able to help edify others, contribute to the body of Christ, and be filled with Christ. Edifying others involves helping them to change. This requires love for them. We must remember that our authority comes from God's Word, and so we must know His Word and seek His guidance. Helping others to change focuses on helping them to mature in Christ and follow the standards in God's Word, not on trying to change their personalities.

Paul teaches that change comes with training: "Exercise yourself toward godliness" (1 Tim. 4:7). Training to meet a goal will bring about results. Change comes when people ask the Holy Spirit for help, repent of sin, are accountable to others, and train in godly behavior. As we seek to edify others and help them mature, we must expose sin, encourage repentance, and instruct in righteousness. We will note change in others' lives when they are learning to live according to God's standards in His Word.

For more on change/maturity, see the article by Ron Hawkins in **The Soul Care Bible**, page 1526 (2 Cor. 5:17).

Child Development

Deuteronomy 4:9

"Only take heed to yourself, and diligently keep yourself, lest you forget the things your eyes have seen, and lest they depart from your heart all the days of your life. And teach them to your children and your grandchildren."

 Christians, whether they are parents or not, are responsible for the guidance and nurture of the children in their lives. God tells us that we should diligently learn His lessons, and then teach our children the lessons that He has taught us.

God created each child with special characteristics. The same mother can give birth to two very different people. Children's characters and identities are based on their unique personalities as created by God, the choices they make, and the environment in which they grow up. Christian parents, teachers, and others who have children in their lives have the awesome privilege and responsibility to love, nurture, and instruct these precious little ones.

Children learn to make decisions by the boundaries, discipline, and consistency maintained by their parents. The family's unconditional love, the bonding of the family members, and strong parental leadership also direct children's decision-making skills. Children need to learn to make their own choices as they grow older. We are raising them so that we can one day let them go out into the world as responsible adults.

For more on child development, see the article by Paul Meier in **The Soul Care Bible**, page 228 (Deut. 4:9, 10).

Child Discipline

Proverbs 22:15

Foolishness is bound up in the heart of a child; the rod of correction will drive it far from him.

 Discipline strategies that work for most kids do not have the same effect on a strong-willed child. The difficult qualities of a strong-willed child do not have to be seen as negative traits, however. Parents can learn to find strengths and possibilities in a strong-willed child without compromising any accountability. Parents need to understand that strong-willed children do not have trouble with authority, but with how it is communicated. A friendly, respectful tone, rather than simply giving orders, is more likely to produce positive results.

Strong-willed children do not want to be controlled. Parents can still experience successful discipline by inspiring, motivating, and holding the child accountable to obedience. Parents must realize that they cannot force obedience, but they can try different approaches. The effectiveness of a parent's discipline strategies will be determined by the quality of their relationship with the child. If the relationship is hostile, the child will not be inclined to obey. If it is a cultivated relationship, the child will be more willing to obey.

No two children are alike. Knowing our child's unique gifts and character traits will help us to discover which approaches to take in parenting a strong-willed child.

For more on child discipline, see the article by Cynthia Ulrich Tobias in **The Soul Care Bible**, page 830 (Prov. 22:15).

Death

2 Kings 20:1

In those days Hezekiah was sick and near death. And Isaiah the prophet, the son of Amoz, went to him and said to him, "Thus says the LORD: 'Set your house in order, for you shall die, and not live.'"

King Hezekiah responded as many of us would if we were told of our impending death. God did not desire for humanity to experience death. Because of sin, however, death entered the world.

Are we prepared to die? The Bible gives us three clear steps in preparing for our eternal future: (1) We must admit that we are sinners and cannot go to heaven when we die—no matter how good we are or how many good deeds we do. (2) We must believe that Jesus Christ died to pay the penalty for our sins in order to save us from eternal punishment. (3) We must tell God that we believe, that we want to confess our sins and accept Christ's sacrifice on our behalf. We must accept that we are sinners and that the only way to heaven is through His Son, Jesus Christ, just as His Word says. Jesus alone is the way, the truth, and the life.

How should believers view death? Our perspective on death affects the way we handle it. Christians should approach death with positive anticipation because we long to be with God forever. Physical pain and suffering are only temporary for Christians. We will finally be home when we enter through the doorway of death to eternal life with God in heaven.

For more on **death**, see the article by Woodrow Kroll in **The Soul Care Bible**, page 500 (2 Kin. 20:1–3).

Decision Making

Romans 12:2

And do not be conformed to this world, but be transformed by the renewing of your mind, that you may prove what is that good and acceptable and perfect will of God.

 When we do not understand God or how He works in our lives, we become confused about knowing or not knowing His will. God is concerned with our becoming like His Son. Understanding this will help us determine His will.

There are two facets of God's will. The first one is His *decretive* will, which is His determined, decreed will. It is absolute, unchangeable, unconditional, and is always in accordance with His plan and His nature. The Bible reveals requirements that are part of God's decretive will for everyone. Some of these include obeying and honoring parents, meditating on the Scriptures, praying, proclaiming Christ, and loving others. The second facet of God's will is His *permissive* will. God allows things, such as sin and suffering, to happen and uses the situation to accomplish His purposes.

We can have a better understanding of God's will when we follow these principles: (1) Look to God's Word, (2) listen to the prompting of the Holy Spirit, (3) seek the counsel of godly people, and (4) look for an inner assurance of peace. Following these principles will renew our minds and help us to better determine God's will for our lives.

For more on decision making, see the article by Charles R. Swindoll in **The Soul Care Bible**, page 1484 (Rom. 12:2).

Depression

Psalm 130:1, 2

Out of the depths I have cried to You, O LORD; Lord, hear my voice! Let Your ears be attentive to the voice of my supplications.

Depression is a deep level of emotional turmoil. It is often caused by fear, loneliness, guilt, or anger. There may also be environmental and medical factors at work as well.

Symptoms of depression may include physical weakness and illness, loss of meaning, loss of appetite, feelings of isolation and rejection, or insomnia. In some people, these symptoms last for great lengths of time. They may need to seek medical treatment. If the symptoms are minor or sporadic, the person can seek other ways to respond to the depression. It helps to be aware, and to have those closest to the person aware, so that help can be given when it is needed.

There are healthy and unhealthy ways to respond to depression. Those who focus on the situation instead of on God may respond in unhealthy ways by refusing to eat, feeling angry toward God, isolating themselves, or sleeping often. Healthy responses include avoiding isolation, being accountable to someone who can help, and staying clear of unhealthy relationships and negative or addictive behaviors. Above all, it is important to seek and accept God's help. The psalmist called from the depths of despair, and God heard him. He hears those who are hurting.

For more on depression, see the article by Michael R. Lyles in **The Soul Care Bible**, page 780 (Ps. 130).

Discouragement

Joshua 1:9

"Have I not commanded you? Be strong and of good courage; do not be afraid, nor be dismayed, for the LORD your God is with you wherever you go."

 When people assess their resources and abilities, they sometimes feel discouraged, especially when a situation seems very difficult. Joshua had to follow in Moses' footsteps, and he had the added responsibility of bringing the nation into the land and conquering it. God told Joshua not to be discouraged, but to trust Him.

Just because a situation seems overwhelming doesn't mean that God is oblivious or that He has lost control. God allows our struggles, knowing that they will push us to grow in maturity and character. These times test our faith and force us to answer the question, "Am I confident of God's unlimited power?" Without that confidence, it is easy to get trapped in discouragement.

At the first feeling of discouragement, Christians should stop and pray. Discouragement will build when we forget God and try to go it alone. When we take time to talk with God, He helps us understand His guidance for the situation. Read God's Word. Claim His promises. Be positive, focus upward, press on, and realize that God will bring you through this situation. "Be strong and of good courage; do not be afraid … God is with you wherever you go."

For more on **discouragement**, see the article by John R. Cheydleur in **The Soul Care Bible**, page 266 (Josh. 1:6–8).

Divorce/Separation

Deuteronomy 24:1

When a man takes a wife and marries her, and it happens that she finds no favor in his eyes because he has found some uncleanness in her, and he writes her a certificate of divorce, puts it in her hand, and sends her out of his house....

Regardless of Christians' desire to nurture and protect their marriages, some do fall to divorce. God understood this and so made laws to protect both parties in the event of a divorce. When Christians find themselves in an unwanted divorce, they are left to recover from a loss they had not expected. The route to a healthy recovery takes time and support. God provides resources, however, to take one the worst events in a person's life and use it for good.

The divorced person will feel very sensitive —words from friends and family, even well-meant, can be very hurtful. It is important for family and friends to take the person under their wings to prevent him or her from making big changes and/or new relationships too quickly. The recovery process takes time— about two to five years. Divorced people experience stages of denial, anger, bargaining with God, depression, and finally, acceptance. Acceptance is the endpoint when the person will finally be able to forgive, pray, and wish the former spouse well.

God can heal the deep wounds of divorce. There *is* life after divorce. The divorced person can take comfort that God is always faithful and will never leave. His love is perfect.

For more on **divorce/separation**, see the article by Tom Whiteman in **The Soul Care Bible**, page 250 (Deut. 24:1–4).

Doubt

John 20:27

Then He said to Thomas, "Reach your finger here, and look at My hands; and reach your hand here, and put it into My side. Do not be unbelieving, but believing."

Several men in the Bible experienced doubt: Job doubted God in his suffering, Abraham was unsure of God's promises, John the Baptist doubted if Jesus was truly the Messiah, Thomas doubted Jesus' resurrection, and Paul struggled with unanswered prayer. These men had dynamic relationships with God that were strengthened, not hindered, by their doubt.

We all struggle with doubt, but in different ways. There are three types of doubt that affect us. *Factual doubt* occurs when people question the solid foundation of Christianity. Such doubt can be handled by giving evidences for Christian truth, as Jesus did for Thomas. *Volitional doubt* is concerned with the will. Those who have this doubt have little desire to follow God. They must be challenged in their loss of motivation to believe the truth. *Emotional doubt* comes from passions and moods. Emotional doubters judge the facts surrounding their beliefs based on their feelings about those beliefs. These doubters must learn to think and practice the truth. Their thinking patterns must be changed before their emotions get involved. They must practice truth by repeating it, writing it down, meditating on it, thanking and praising God, praying, and remembering His promises.

For more on **doubt**, see the article by Gary R. Habermas in **The Soul Care Bible**, page 1408 (John 20:24–29).

Drug Abuse

Ecclesiastes 2:3

I searched in my heart how to gratify my flesh with wine, while guiding my heart with wisdom, and how to lay hold on folly, till I might see what was good for the sons of men to do under heaven all the days of their lives.

People use substances to avoid or ease pain and to find pleasure. Even King Solomon understood that wine could give great gratification; too much wine (or too much of anything), however, and one falls into folly.

Substance disorders affect all areas of society. An estimated 10 percent of the population of any community in the United States could be diagnosed with a substance disorder. And many more substance abusers go undetected. Substance *abuse* is when someone uses a substance excessively in order to cope with stress. Substance *addiction* is when someone depends on a substance in order to function. Addiction affects every aspect of a person's life. Substance abusers will exhibit behaviors of denial, anger, guilt, frustration, and fear when facing their own addictions. They behave this way in order to avoid responsibility for getting help.

Treatment of a substance disorder must involve individual and family therapy. Those with disorders must identify their needs and communicate openly with their families. God, through His Word, promises to help His people through any situation. Abusers must choose between continuing to use the substance to avoid pain and seeking spiritual resources for recovery. Christians are encouraged to persevere through trials so God can work in their lives.

For more on drug abuse, see the article by Mark Shadoan in **The Soul Care Bible**, page 852 (Eccl. 2:1–3).

Eating Disorders

Judges 3:17

So he brought the tribute to Eglon king of Moab. (Now Eglon was a very fat man.)

 King Eglon had an eating disorder—he had allowed himself to become very fat. That is one kind of disorder; other types of disorders occur when people are obsessed about being thin.

To the people with eating disorders such as anorexia or bulimia, the abuse of their bodies may not seem harmful at all. The obsession to become thin affects every part of their lives. A few symptoms for both anorexia and bulimia include secretive behavior coupled with trips to the bathroom after eating, depression, social withdrawal, and a preoccupation with body weight and appearance. They may think that they are fat even when they are extremely thin. We need to be alert to symptoms of these diseases so we can intervene. The anorexic or bulimic will need our help, and we should do everything we can to help, for these diseases can be deadly if left untreated.

Helping the anorexic or bulimic is not easy. The sick person must desire to be better before any progress can be made. Love and patience will be required. The sick person needs to understand that he or she is beautiful to God. Prayer, patience, and acceptance will go a long way toward healing.

For more on **eating disorders**, see the article by Jesse Dillinger and Gregory L. Jantz in **The Soul Care Bible**, page 302 (Judg. 3:17).

Emotional Life

Lamentations 3:22, 23

Through the LORD's mercies we are not consumed, because His compassions fail not. They are new every morning; great is Your faithfulness.

 A healthy faith is the foundation of healthy emotions. In the middle of Jeremiah's lament over how badly he was being treated by the people to whom he was prophesying, he spoke these powerful words about God's compassion and faithfulness. Jeremiah's circumstances were terrible, but he new that God's compassions never fail. Thus, Jeremiah could remain strong. When we have faith in God and His compassion, when we know of His mercy, we will be able to handle anything that comes our way. This gives us emotional health.

In order to gain and maintain emotional health, we need to see ourselves as God sees us. In His eyes we are valuable, loveable, forgivable, and changeable. It helps to maintain a correct perspective on difficulties, react appropriately, and willingly face growth and change. It is important to participate in endeavors of eternal significance, such as close relationships, giving generously, and learning to understand and experience God's love.

Of course we will face times when the hurts seem overwhelming. We can follow Jeremiah's example by talking honestly to God and asking Him to help us and to give us a new perspective on our situation. God's compassions never fail; they are new each day.

For more on emotional life, see the article by Richard Dobbins in **The Soul Care Bible**, page 1040 (Lam. 3).

Eternal Life

Revelation 21:22

But I saw no temple in it, for the Lord God Almighty and the Lamb are its temple.

 People of all religions have hope of living eternally in a better place after death. Christians and Jews, however, are the only ones who know about heaven because God has told us about it in His Word.

Jesus spoke about heaven when He was on earth. He promised to take all those who believe in Him to His "Father's house," where God dwells (John 14:1-3). The book of Revelation gives the following descriptions of heaven: God will be with His people; it will be a place of eternal joy; its beauty is indescribable; God is heaven's focal point; the river of life runs through it; the tree of life grows there; heaven is only for those who accepted Christ as Savior.

Jesus died for the sins of all mankind, yet only those have accepted Christ as Savior will see heaven. We can only receive forgiveness and salvation through Christ, because He alone died on the cross for our sins. We do not know when Christ will return, but we do know that He will come. Because of this, we must share our faith with others, so that they may also accept Christ and live eternally with Him in heaven.

For more on eternal life, see the article by Tim LaHaye in **The Soul Care Bible**, page 1718 (Rev. 21:22).

Failure

2 Chronicles 36:19

Then they burned the house of God, broke down the wall of Jerusalem, burned all its palaces with fire, and destroyed all its precious possessions.

 God's people had failed—miserably. They had been promised greatness, but their disobedience led to disaster. Failure, however, is not always the end. God can use failure to draw believers closer to Himself. Failure teaches in ways that success cannot. When Christians go through times of failure, they find a new perspective of God as the powerful, almighty God who is in control. God does not abandon those who fail. He understands that His people are weak. People in the Bible such as Adam and Eve, Moses, Abraham, David, Elijah, Jonah, and Peter all failed at times. Yet God forgave them and continued to use them for His service. God hates sin, but He can use the circumstances of failure to bring people to the cross.

Christians must ask God to help them have a proper perspective of failure and have the ability to learn from it. The focus should not be on the failure itself. Instead, failures should be used as stepping stones to a deeper relationship with God. Because of God's forgiveness and acceptance, a Christian can still be successful in His sight. His grace covers the failures and transforms them.

For more on failure, see the article by Gary J. Oliver in **The Soul Care Bible**, page 586 (2 Chr. 36).

Faith

Hebrews 11:6

But without faith it is impossible to please Him,
for he who comes to God must believe that He
is, and that He is a rewarder of those who diligently seek Him.

Faith is ultimately an act of trust
in which we commit to someone
or something. For Christians,
faith is belief based on the confidence of God's promises. This
involves recognizing God's revealed truth and
surrendering to Him. Faith in Jesus Christ and
in His atoning death is at the center of the
Christian life.

Salvation is received by grace, through faith
(Eph. 2:8). Christ is the object of our faith, and
it is through Him that we experience forgiveness. We could not have attained salvation for
ourselves.

Faith allows us to please God, and we are
rewarded by God for seeking Him (Heb. 11:6).
There is a general correlation between our
faith in God and His response to our prayers
(Matt. 5:34; 7:7). We cannot, however, make
God give a "yes" answer to our prayers offered
in faith.

As James explains, faith and works are linked
(James 2:14-24). Through faith we have salvation, whereas good works are the signs of our
salvation. We cannot be saved by our works,
but only by what Jesus has done for us.

A faith that is real will produce righteous
works. The way a person lives will be evidence
of a saving knowledge of Jesus Christ.

For more on faith, see the article by Jerry Falwell in **The
Soul Care Bible**, page 1634 (Heb. 11:6).

Family Life

Joshua 24:15

"And if it seems evil to you to serve the LORD, choose for yourselves this day whom you will serve, whether the gods which your fathers served that were on the other side of the River, or the gods of the Amorites, in whose land you dwell. But as for me and my house, we will serve the LORD."

 Maintaining a strong, loving family takes work. After one's relationship with God, the family relationship is top priority. The family is the source of self-worth, love, satisfaction, and meaning. Families are blessed by God. The husband and wife are joined by God, and the children are products of that love. God created the family and meant it to contain the strongest relationships.

To nurture a strong family life, we need to promote strong commitments, which will create a sense of security and love. Family members should never need to doubt one another's commitment and care. For believers, the family should be as it was for Joshua—a place where the family members learn about, talk about, and serve the Lord.

Out of such commitment and security will come family members who feel appreciated. They will feel that if they were to leave the family, they would be missed and no one could replace them. Communicating love and respect will maintain that sense of appreciation and security. Family members can communicate their commitment, love, and respect through words of appreciation and quality time together. Families who promote this kind of atmosphere are very blessed indeed.

For more on family life, see the article by Nick Stinnett in **The Soul Care Bible**, page 294 (Josh. 24:15).

Family Problems

Genesis 25:28

And Isaac loved Esau because he ate of his game, but Rebekah loved Jacob.

 All families face problems. Yet when a family is embroiled in a difficult problem, it may feel as though it is the only family to ever have to face such difficulty. But family problems go all the way back to Adam and Eve. In the story in Genesis 25, family problems occurred between Isaac's sons because of obvious favoritism by the parents.

In any case, family problems may not always be easily fixed. How the problem is defined, and who is blamed, will determine the solutions that are attempted. Although some solutions may give a temporary reprieve, often difficult problems need a different approach.

A family may need to take the time to discover and consider patterns that have been occurring over time, a pattern that may have been in place for years or generations. Then the family will need to face the truth and determine what types of actions and attitudes can break longstanding patterns. Finally, a family can work through the difficult steps of forgiveness and reconciliation in order to put the past behind and move ahead. Resolving to take these steps can bring healing and change to a family.

To read more on family problems, see the article by David Stoop in **The Soul Care Bible**, page 38 (Gen. 25).

Fatherhood

I Chronicles 3:1

Now these were the sons of David who were born to him in Hebron: The firstborn was Amnon, by Ahinoam the Jezreelitess; the second, Daniel, by Abigail the Carmelitess....

 In order for a man to be a great father, he must always love and serve his wife first. Once he has set that priority straight, he needs to build the following game plan to be a successful dad. King David had many sons, but he could have used this advice!

A great dad guards his children physically when they are young and emotionally as they grow and mature. He communicates. The most precious gift a father can give his children is the art of conversation. A dad must listen with both his ears and his eyes. A dad must also hold his children. His touch communicates security and worth to his children's hearts. He must also be willing to discipline his children when needed. Children have confidence in discipline when their father's life is modeled by self-discipline. Great dads know how to laugh and have fun with their kids.

Christian dads are true treasures. When a dad is saved through the power of Jesus Christ and lives his faith before his family, nothing is ever the same again. His family is truly blessed. His faith will affect his conduct. A man with good conduct will produce good fruit in his children.

For more on fatherhood, see the article by Robert Wolgemuth in **The Soul Care Bible**, page 516 (I Chr. 3:1).

Fear/Fear of God

Proverbs 1:7

The fear of the LORD is the beginning of knowledge, but fools despise wisdom and instruction.

 The fear of God is a recurring theme throughout Scripture. Deuteronomy 10:12 says that the Lord required Israel to both fear and love Him. Fear and love are physiological opposites. When a person experiences fear, the nervous system's "fight or flight" response kicks in. The body becomes quickly prepared to fight the object or run from it. When a person experiences love, preparation is made to draw near and enjoy. What does it mean, then, to both love *and* fear God?

Other words for fear include reverence, awe, dread, terror, and respect. All are appropriate when thinking about God. He is to be revered; He is indeed awesome beyond all our imaginings, and those who turn away from Him will face terror at His wrath; we have awe-inspired respect for His greatness. To those who believe, God is the ultimate Friend. Through His Son's death, He showed His love. That love inspires us to love Him in return.

Our fear of God should cause us to desire not to displease Him, and to know that He is great and beyond our imaginings. Our love for God should cause us to run from evil, rebellion, or compromise, knowing that we can run straight into His arms.

For more on fear/fear of God, see the article by Gary W. Moon in **The Soul Care Bible**, page 800 (Prov. 1:7).

52

Forgiveness

2 Corinthians 2:10

Now whom you forgive anything, I also forgive. For if indeed I have forgiven anything, I have forgiven that one for your sakes in the presence of Christ.

Emotions such as resentment, bitterness, hatred, hostility, anger, and fear well up in a person who has been hurt by the sin of another. These emotions can lead to unforgiveness. Forgiveness, in contrast, occurs when these emotions of unforgiveness are changed to loving, compassionate, altruistic emotions. This change happens when the heart is transformed by having experienced the love and forgiveness of God.

There are different ways to forgive someone. Those who need to forgive must learn to have empathy for the person who hurt them, have humility about their own sinfulness, and have gratitude because they have experienced God's forgiveness. A way to be able to "reach" out and forgive or to help others forgive is to remember this acrostic:

R = *Recall* the hurt.
E = *Empathize* with the one who caused the hurt.
A = Give an *Altruistic* gift of forgiveness.
C = *Commit* to forgive.
H = *Hold on* to forgiveness.

For more on **forgiveness**, see the article by Everett L. Worthington, Jr. in **The Soul Care Bible**, page 1520 (2 Cor. 2:5–11).

Genetic Issues

Exodus 4:11

So the LORD said to him, "Who has made man's mouth? Or who makes the mute, the deaf, the seeing, or the blind? Have not I, the LORD?"

 Many people aren't satisfied with the way God created them. They've inherited their parents' disability, disease, or deformity, and these genetic disabilities appear to be holding them back from some challenge or accomplishment.

Both Moses and Paul struggled with disabilities that they considered to be handicaps to their ministries. Moses did not feel confident to approach Pharaoh with his slow speech. In Exodus 4, Moses said that this made him a bad choice to go to Pharaoh. God assured Moses, however, that He was in control. We read in the New Testament that the Apostle Paul struggled with a "thorn in his flesh." Paul wanted God to remove it so that his ministry would be more effective. God did not take away the "thorn," but gave Paul the grace to endure. God used both men, however, to do great things for His glory.

God did not forget about their disabilities, but He did not heal them. They served God with their weaknesses. Whatever weaknesses people have today, they can trust that God can and will use them to build His Kingdom. Christians should focus on the power of God to work through those weaknesses to bring Him glory.

To read more on genetic issues, see the article by Michael R. Lyles in **The Soul Care Bible**, page 84 (Ex. 4:11).

God's Promises

Deuteronomy 1:8

"See, I have set the land before you; go in and possess the land which the LORD swore to your fathers—to Abraham, Isaac, and Jacob—to give to them and their descendants after them."

 God always keeps His promises. When the nation of Israel stood poised to enter the promised land, they were witnessing the fulfillment of a promise made to Abraham, Isaac, and Jacob hundreds of years before.

God never forgets. He makes promises and always keeps them. Some promises in the Bible are conditional. That is, the fulfillment of the promise is conditional upon the acts of people. For example, God promised to always keep His people in that land *as long as they obeyed Him*. When the people disobeyed, they went into exile. Other promises, however, are unconditional, meaning they will always be true. For example, the promise that "whoever calls on the name of the LORD shall be saved" (Romans 10:13) is a promise that is always true. God will never rescind His offer of salvation to those who believe—even though many will refuse it.

At times, it is difficult to trust in God's promises. It takes effort to believe in an unseen God. Just as we are faithful to believe, He is faithful to follow through on His word. When we have the courage to believe, we are greatly blessed as we become closer to our Lord.

For more on God's promises, see the article by James Clinton in **The Soul Care Bible**, page 220 (Deut. 1:8–11).

Gossip

Proverbs 26:20, 22

Where there is no wood, the fire goes out; and where there is no talebearer, strife ceases.... The words of a talebearer are like tasty trifles, and they go down into the inmost body.

 Gossip, in the form of rumors, opinions, and "inside" information, is alluring because of its sensational subject matter regarding another's personal issues. Proverbs calls it a "tasty trifle."

Gossipers are motivated by several things. The idea of having the inside scoop makes one feel important, whether it involves gossiping or listening to gossip. It can be flattering to have another share this type of information with us. Gossip is one way of cutting others down, which is often done to make people feel better about themselves. Listening to gossip is dangerous because it associates the listener with the gossip. Gossip is a waste of time. It can color one's judgment about someone; it passes along information that may be incorrect and hurtful. Proverbs is correct in describing the strife gossip can cause.

A helpful way to respond to gossip is by acting disinterested in it. The one who is the object of the gossip can respond either by ignoring it or talking to others to set the record straight; in any case, he or she should be gracious. If we have a problem with gossip, we should ask others to hold us accountable in order to discontinue further gossiping.

For more on gossip, see the article by Dianna Booher in **The Soul Care Bible**, page 838 (Prov. 26:20–26).

Grief/Loss

Isaiah 53:3, 4

He is despised and rejected by men, a Man of sorrows and acquainted with grief.... Surely He has borne our griefs and carried our sorrows.

 The way in which people respond to loss affects them for the rest of their lives. Loss must be seen in the correct perspective so people experiencing it can understand it and deal with it. When people hide their feelings, this only causes more problems. People who experience loss must learn to move on by going through the grieving process.

Grief, although a painful process, is a healthy response to loss and is necessary in order for healing to occur. The first stage in the grief process is denial. People who suffer from loss feel numb. The next stage is when people release emotion, such as anger about the loss, to others and to God. Next, those experiencing grief will struggle with feelings of guilt and anger and won't know how to move on with life. The final stage is acceptance of the loss. They do this by reorganizing their lives and learning how to feel and express their pain.

Jesus experienced loss and grief, so He could identify with us and die in our place. We will not be able to avoid loss and grief in our lives, but we must remember that God is with us through it all.

For more on grief/loss, see the article by H. Norman Wright in **The Soul Care Bible**, page 940 (Is. 53:3, 4).

Guilt/Shame

Ezra 9:6

And I said: "O my God, I am too ashamed and humiliated to lift up my face to You, my God; for our iniquities have risen higher than our heads, and our guilt has grown up to the heavens.

Everyone experiences guilt. And nearly everyone reacts to guilt with feelings of shame. It is important to understand the difference between *feeling* guilty and *being* guilty. Actual guilt is the result of a violation of a moral law. Just *feeling* guilty does not mean we have broken a law. Many people, because of strong emotions, carry guilt they never earned or deserved. Satan is "the accuser" (Rev. 12:10), who works to create feelings of condemnation and guilt for believers. He knows that this can make believers ineffective and immature in their faith—and he loves that! The Holy Spirit, however, works to convict, forgive, and restore.

There are six steps in dealing with guilty feelings: (1) Pay attention to feelings of guilt. (2) Find out the nature and cause of the feelings. (3) Correct the mistakes and move on. (4) Ask God for forgiveness if there is sin. (5) In most cases, confess only to those affected by the sin. (6) If the feelings of guilt are unrealistic, ask God for strength to get rid of them.

Because Christ did not come to condemn us, we should not suffer under self-condemnation. Christ came to set us free from sin and guilt—for eternity.

For more on **guilt/shame**, see the article by Les Parrott in **The Soul Care Bible**, page 600 (Ezra 9:5–8).

Healing/Recovery

James 5:14

Is anyone among you sick? Let him call for the elders of the church, and let them pray over him, anointing him with oil in the name of the Lord.

 Everyone is born into sin and suffers pain, sickness, and difficulties. People are broken by their own sin and the sins of others, and sometimes that brokenness causes them to alienate themselves from others and from God. Broken people need God's healing that only comes from a renewed relationship with Him and with others. Jesus suffered and became broken because of our sin. We are reconciled to God when we accept Jesus' sacrifice for us.

When we accept Christ's sacrifice for our sins, we are considered righteous before God. But this does not mean that we will not experience pain and suffering. We will not be completely free of pain until we reach heaven. We all will continue to struggle with the sinful nature while still on this earth, and we must daily come to God for healing.

Christians are encouraged to pray over sick people and ask God for healing (James 5:14), but this does not guarantee healing. God may choose not to heal in order to help others and to glorify Himself. He may allow us to suffer in order that we might join Christ in His suffering and bring glory to God through it. For when we are weak, He is strong (2 Cor. 12:10).

For more on healing/recovery, see the article by Dan Allender in **The Soul Care Bible**, page 1652 (James 5:14).

Health/Spirituality

2 Samuel 12:20

So David arose from the ground, washed and anointed himself, and changed his clothes; and he went into the house of the LORD and worshiped. Then he went to his own house; and when he requested, they set food before him, and he ate.

David had sinned, but once he got himself back with God and experienced God's discipline, he was able to move on with life. The Bible reveals that obedience to God yields life and peace, while disobedience leads to death. Life lived in Christ leads to good health, as research has shown.

Scientists have learned that high levels of religious commitment and church participation lead to reduced suicidal behavior, reduced drug abuse, and less depression. Religious commitment has also been shown to lessen distress, give a greater sense of well-being, and result in fewer psychiatric symptoms. In addition, higher levels of religious commitment produce healthier lifestyles, are related to lower blood pressure levels and reduced hypertension, and reduce the death rate for males and females. Studies have also shown that as religious commitment increases, there are greater levels of marital satisfaction, women are more satisfied with their sexual lives, and divorce rates are reduced.

Religion affects physical health. Those who live an intrinsic faith, internalizing and living out their beliefs, live healthier lives. Life lived daily in Christ gives the believer the assurance of salvation and eternal life, which leads to good health.

For more on health/spirituality, see the article by George Ohlschlager in **The Soul Care Bible**, page 402 (2 Sam. 12:1–23).

Homosexuality

Romans 1:26, 27

Their women exchanged the natural use for what is against nature. Likewise also the men ... burned in their lust for one another, men with men committing what is shameful, and receiving in themselves the penalty of their error which was due.

The homosexual *condition*, or orientation, refers to the sexual attraction a person has for members of the same sex. Homosexual *behavior* refers to any sexual activity between members of the same sex. While people do not usually choose the homosexual condition, they *can* choose their behavior.

There is no solid evidence that homosexuality is inborn. Studies have shown that the homosexual condition is a result of a need for intimacy with members of the same sex. This can be caused by a faulty relationship with the same-sex parent, lack of bonding with peers, or sexual abuse.

God condemns all forms of sexual behavior outside of marriage, as well as those homosexual activities (Rom. 1:32). Both the Old Testament and the New Testament speak of homosexuality as being an "abomination" (Lev. 18:22) or "shameful" (Rom. 1:24-27). Yet even in Paul's time, God delivered people from this sin.

If someone we love is homosexual, we can remind them of God's standards and of our love. We must accept those we love even when we don't approve of their sinful behavior. Even when our efforts to change them fail, God's power is greater. There is hope for deliverance.

For more on homosexuality, see the article by Joe Dallas in **The Soul Care Bible**, page 1466 (Rom. 1:27).

Honor

Esther 6:6

So Haman came in, and the king asked him, "What shall be done for the man whom the king delights to honor?" Now Haman thought in his heart, "Whom would the king delight to honor more than me?"

 Haman thought he deserved great honor—but the king was seeking to honor one who truly deserved such praise. When we show honor to another person, we are communicating his or her value to us. As a lighthouse provides security, hope, and safety to wayward vessels, so honor provides security, hope, and safety in relationships.

Honor is one of the most important elements in a marriage. Honoring your spouse means putting love into action. You can begin by recognizing that your spouse is a treasure, a gift from God to you. Then you must treat him/her that way—as worthy of praise. When you see your spouse as a treasure, you will inevitably focus more on his or her positives instead of on the negatives. You can notice and mention what you love, appreciate, and enjoy about your spouse.

Showing honor to others builds a great foundation for any relationship. In marriage, it is especially important for each spouse to put into practice the acts that show honor to each other. When you do this, you are providing security, hope, and a safe harbor in life's storms.

For more on honor, see the article by Gary Smalley and Greg Smalley in **The Soul Care Bible**, page 630 (Esth. 6:6).

Joy

Nehemiah 8:10

Then he said to them, "Go your way, eat the fat, drink the sweet, and send portions to those for whom nothing is prepared; for this day is holy to our Lord. Do not sorrow, for the joy of the LORD is your strength."

 God intends for us to experience joy and laughter. Laughing is an expression of joy that comes from God. Did you ever think about the fact that humor encourages and edifies the church? God enjoys humor and loves to see us enjoying it as well. There is a difference, however, between worldly humor and godly humor. Worldly humor glorifies sin, puts others down, ridicules righteousness, and hurts the spirit. Godly humor avoids offense, builds others up, honors God, and heals the spirit.

Laughter brings both emotional and physical healing. Laughing at ourselves shows that we have maturity, healthy self-esteem, and right priorities. When we laugh, we heal emotionally. Laughter has been proven to heal people physically as well. Laughter relaxes the body, reduces pain, increases our ability to cope with life, massages the organs, exercises the facial muscles, increases the heart rate and improves circulation, gives oxygen to the body, and stimulates the immune system. Clearly, laughter is a great help to us in life! When we can laugh, we can really live.

For the Christian, laughter is something we can take with us forever. When we die with Christ in our hearts, we know we will live and laugh with Him for eternity.

For more on joy, see the article by Liz Curtis Higgs in **The Soul Care Bible**, page 614 (Neh. 8:10).

Judgmentalism

Luke 6:37

"Judge not, and you shall not be judged. Condemn not, and you shall not be condemned. Forgive, and you will be forgiven."

 There is a difference between *judging* and being *judgmental.* Christians should judge between good and evil in order to discern God's will. They should also judge sin in order to deal with it (1 Cor. 5:1-12).

Jesus clearly said, however, that we are not to judge and condemn others. Those who do so become judgmental people who are critical, condescending, unloving, unforgiving, self-centered, and focused more on other's mistakes than on helping them. Such people usually do not have intimate relationships and find it difficult to share their feelings. Critical people usually relate to people in a parental-style role, which often makes them uneasy. Shame is also used as a method of trying to control others.

Two causes of judgmentalism are guilt and fear. People may feel guilty and criticize others for the same problems with which they themselves struggle, or they may criticize others out of fear when they do not understand them.

Praying for others and being involved in an accountability relationship where judgmentalism is addressed are ways to break free from the habit. We should be quick to remember that ultimate judgment belongs to God alone (Rev. 20:11-15).

For more on judgmentalism, see the article by Ed Hindson in **The Soul Care Bible**, page 1324 (Luke 6:37, 38).

Knowing God

Leviticus 26:12

"I will walk among you and be your God, and you shall be My people."

 Who is God, exactly? Many people treat Him as though He exists merely to fix all their problems. Others question His existence. Others treat Him like a cosmic catalog to whom they can place their orders and get whatever they want. Still others think about Him only in times of hardship—sometimes to blame Him, at other times to seek His help.

Times of hardship may be just the key to bringing some people to an understanding of their need for God. Turning to God in times of hardship is legitimate because He loves us. Yet, He is far more than just a "Right Hand Man." He is our God, the God whom we worship. Christianity is not about Christians; it's about God. We exist for Him, not He for us. We live to glorify Him. Our greatest desire should be to get to know Him through a personal relationship with Jesus Christ.

Knowing God means feeling a passion to concentrate on God, not our own problems. We are to be steadfast with a single-minded determination to know Him and His character. That is what it means to find God: trusting Jesus to reveal God when we put our faith in His hands.

For more on knowing God, see the article by Larry Crabb in **The Soul Care Bible**, page 164 (Lev. 26:9–13).

Knowing Jesus

John 1:29

The next day John saw Jesus coming toward him, and said, "Behold! The Lamb of God who takes away the sin of the world!"

 The primary figure of the Bible is Jesus. The Old Testament tells of His coming, and the New Testament tells of His life on the earth and what He is now doing for us in heaven. The name Jesus means "Savior," and Christ means "Messiah." He is the promised Messiah of the Old Testament, who brings hope to the hopeless and offers us God's salvation, love, and grace.

Jesus is depicted in four different ways in the Gospels. He is pictured as the King of the Jews in Matthew, as the Servant of the Lord in Mark, as the Son of Man in Luke, and as the Son of God in John. He performed miracles and shared brilliant teachings. He healed the sick, raised the dead, fed the hungry, and loved the outcasts. He is the perfect and complete picture of God.

Jesus died on the cross as sufficient payment for our sins (1 Cor. 15:1-4). Believing this means we recognize Him as our Savior and accept God's offer of eternal life. To believe in Jesus means that we affirm by faith that what He did on the cross is enough. In believing, we are saved (Rom. 10:13).

For more on knowing Jesus, see the article by Ed Hindson in **The Soul Care Bible**, page 1368 (John 1:29).

Legalism

Leviticus 11:45

For I am the LORD who brings you up out of the land of Egypt, to be your God. You shall therefore be holy, for I am holy.

 God requires holiness from His people, but that holiness cannot be obtained by obeying rules. Holiness is given by God to His people (1 Cor. 1:2). On the opposite side is legalism—the idea that rigid rules are the routes to salvation. Often, these rules are made by Christians. These are not taken from God's Word, but made up on their own and then placed upon people as though they *were* God's Word. Legalists believe that breaking those rules means a person is not a believer. They make works (rule-keeping) more important than grace and freedom in Christ. However, rule-keeping doesn't save anyone. While good works should be a natural outcome of our faith, they are not required in order to be saved.

Too often, legalism gets in the way of Christian relationships. When Christians cannot tolerate others' personal rules, there are problems. Believers should tolerate one another's personal convictions. But it is inappropriate when those convictions are used to determine whether someone is saved. It is only by grace that we are saved.

Refocusing on God's love is the best way to prevent lawful condemnation. His free gift of salvation puts the Holy Spirit in our hearts and gives us freedom in Christ.

For more on legalism, see the article by Dan Mitchell in **The Soul Care Bible**, page 142 (Lev. 11).

Life Transitions

1 Chronicles 23:1

So when David was old and full of days, he made his son Solomon king over Israel.

 David had slain a giant in his youth, had become a great warrior and king, and then, in his old age, he gave the kingdom to his son. Life transitions are important changes that everyone experiences. We can resist these changes, or we can allow these changes to transform us. It is healthy and necessary to recognize the changes and their role in our personal development. If we learn how to navigate through the transitions in life, we will become the people God intended us to be. Because life transitions signal an end and a beginning, we must allow ourselves to grieve our endings and be encouraged by new beginnings.

There are four steps in handling life transitions. First, we must accept that life transitions are inevitable. The second step is to allow the change to work in our lives to help us become who we were meant to be. We need to trust that God is in control. Next, we must have perseverance through the difficult times. Character is developed when we persevere through painful changes. Finally, we must trust in God's purposes for our lives and patiently wait for them to unfold.

For more on life transitions, see the article by Freda V. Crews in **The Soul Care Bible**, page 540 (1 Chr. 23).

Loneliness

Psalm 69:8

I have become a stranger to my brothers, and an alien to my mother's children.

 Humans need intimacy with God and with people. Genuine intimacy with God was lost when sin entered the Garden. Therefore, loneliness came to inhabit the human race.

Loneliness occurs when people desire intimacy but don't receive it. It is an emotional response to being alone. *Physical separation* causes situational loneliness. Loneliness due to brief separation may increase the joy of the reunion, while loneliness due to extensive separation (such as death) is harder to deal with. *Emotional separation* also causes loneliness. People often feel lonely when surrounded by those with whom they have no intimacy. *Chronic loneliness* occurs when people feel they don't belong or are not understood. These feelings can lead to suicide or angry alienation.

In order to deal with loneliness, the source of the loneliness must be identified. If it is due to a perception, then the perception can be changed. If it is due to a real circumstance, the lonely person must learn to accept the situation. The best way to overcome loneliness is by serving others in need. Loneliness helps people through the grieving process. It can also bring people closer to God and to others.

For more on **loneliness**, see article by Miriam Stark Parent in **The Soul Care Bible**, page 734 (Ps. 69:1–8).

Love

I Corinthians 13:13

And now abide faith, hope, love, these three; but the greatest of these is love.

Doing good to those who sin against us could be called "bold love." Such love actively pursues an offender in order to reconcile by exposing the need for confession, repentance, and restoration.

The description of love found in 1 Corinthians 13 includes characteristics such as "kind," "not puffed up," "does not seek its own," "endures all things," and "never fails." Love is not vengeful, but it humbles those who injure by doing good. Bold love is returning evil with good so that evil is destroyed and the heart is redeemed.

We are not just to forgive those who violate us, but we are to serve them. This act of bold love is both unnerving and disarming. The power from God to show kindness surprises and shames those who have harmed us. God uses love to destroy the power of darkness.

Our love of others should be both strong and tender. Love's strength shows God's hatred of sin, while tenderness displays His grace and reconciliation. Bold love does all it can to pursue reconciliation. It will change both our hearts and the hearts of those who hurt us.

For more on love, see the article by Dan Allender in **The Soul Care Bible**, page 1512 (1 Cor. 13).

Love Languages

1 John 4:12

No one has seen God at any time. If we love one another, God abides in us, and His love has been perfected in us.

Falling in love is a temporary, romantic, emotional obsession. *Staying* in love means a couple keeps the warm emotions alive, and this is a challenge. The Bible refers to "love" as an attitude and behavior. If we want to keep love alive, we must choose to have the attitude of love by looking out for the other's interest first. Loving behavior follows the choice to love. We don't deserve God's love, but He chooses to love us even though we are sinners. We need to follow His example.

Everyone has a need to be loved, but each person has a primary love language in which he or she needs to be shown that love. There are five love languages: words of affirmation, gifts, acts of service, quality time, and physical touch. We need to learn what the primary love language is for our spouse and for our children in order to meet their emotional needs.

We can find out what the primary love language of our spouse or children is by paying attention to how they express love, what they complain about, and what they request. These actions often reveal the way they want to receive love.

For more on love languages, see the article by Gary D. Chapman in **The Soul Care Bible**, page 1680 (1 John 4:12).

Marital Communication

1 Peter 3:1, 7

Wives, likewise, be submissive to your own husbands, that even if some do not obey the word, they, without a word, may be won by the conduct of their wives.... Husbands, likewise, dwell with them with understanding, giving honor to the wife....

Effective communication builds intimacy in a marriage. Most couples who seek counseling do so because of poor communication in their marriage. All married couples can learn to improve the quality of their communication.

Perfect communication occurs when the intent of a verbal or written message that is sent and received is fully understood by the receiver. Perfect communication is rarely attained. Imperfect communication, on the other hand, occurs often due to distractions and misunderstandings.

Many couples lack quality communication because they do not spend enough time together. These couples must learn to *choose* to spend time in conversation. They should determine what their priorities should be and avoid becoming overloaded with other commitments. Couples should make time to talk with each other by not allowing other activities to completely fill their schedule.

Discussions between couples should be filled with honesty, respect, and most of all, love (1 Pet. 3:8). Couples need to learn to communicate purposefully, and each person must learn to become a good listener. Listening is key to quality communication.

For more on marital communication, see the article by Tim and Julie Clinton in **The Soul Care Bible**, page 1660 (1 Peter 3:1–9).

Marital Problems

Colossians 3:18, 19

Wives, submit to your own husbands, as is fitting in the Lord. Husbands, love your wives and do not be bitter toward them.

 Every marriage has periods where love and closeness are lacking. Usually, a pattern of relating can be found that can help us understand where the trouble started. Through some work, these harmful patterns can be reversed and a marriage can be given new life.

Everyday pressures are heavily responsible for the beginning of marital dissatisfaction. Selfishness can be a problem. Sometimes one spouse will take advantage of the other, and both end up hurt. The only remedy is to be honest, seek forgiveness, and invest more in the other. Stress is another factor, so couples must identify which stresses affect them. Satan loves to create wedges in every marriage by magnifying weaknesses and fears. Each spouse also needs to remember that only God can perfectly fulfill a person's needs. Spouses should deal with each other's flaws with humility, grace, and forgiveness. Sometimes the past creeps in and causes problems. Childhood scripts, such as abandonment, abuse, or divorce need to be dealt with before God to keep the past from infecting one's marriage. Finally, to keep a marriage strong, spouses must be deliberate about spending time together.

When couples do these things, they are well on their way to marital problem solving.

For more on marital problems, see the article by Tim Clinton in **The Soul Care Bible**, page 1576 (Col. 3:18, 19).

Marriage

Mark 10:6-8

"But from the beginning of the creation, God 'made them male and female.' 'For this reason a man shall leave his father and mother and be joined to his wife, and the two shall become one flesh'; so then they are no longer two, but one flesh."

 Under the Old Covenant, the sacrifice of animals and the sprinkling of blood were used as atonement for sin. Under the New Covenant, the death of Jesus and His blood was the ultimate sacrifice for sin. God's covenants are His promises to us. That is why He established marriage as a covenant between a man and wife. Through the example of marriage, God displays His commitment to love us forever. God created marriage to join a man and a woman as "one flesh." In a covenant marriage, two people "become one." Their two wills must die so that one may be born. A covenant marriage is for life, and it is not to be broken except in cases of adultery or death. God takes the breaking of the marriage covenant very seriously (Mal. 2:13-16). He holds marriage partners accountable for the vows they make to each other.

Marriage is the most sacred and most sacrificial of all relationships. There cannot be covenant without sacrifice. The two who "become one" must learn to surrender their own wills and not allow selfishness to take over. Selfishness is the underlying cause of all marital conflicts; unselfishness, however, leads to happy marriages.

For more on marriage, see the article by Fred Lowery in **The Soul Care Bible**, page 1296 (Mark 10:1–12).

Men's Issues

I Timothy 6:11

But you, O man of God, flee these things and pursue righteousness, godliness, faith, love, patience, gentleness.

 An authentic man honestly and accurately views himself and the world around him. Part of viewing oneself honestly means understanding that feelings are part of being a man. An authentic man experiences his feelings honestly and consciously. Instead of ignoring his feelings, he responds to them, processes them, and evaluates them by acting on them responsibly.

Men become authentic when they cultivate a relationship with God. They must draw close to Him daily and depend on Him to help with decisions and daily pressures of life. Men must also cultivate relationships with other men. Jesus was transparent with His disciples and shared a deep relationship with them.

Authentic men are leaders. Leadership involves mentoring others by example. Authentic men must live by pursuing righteousness, godliness, faith, love, patience, and gentleness. A leader helps others in need and helps others become leaders through discipleship and sharing God's grace with them. God uses the difficulties in men's lives to strengthen them so they can serve and lead others.

For more on men's issues, see the article by Rod Cooper in The Soul Care Bible, page 1600 (1 Tim. 6:11).

Mental Illness

I Samuel 16:14

But the Spirit of the LORD departed from Saul, and a distressing spirit from the LORD troubled him.

 Everyone goes through periods of trouble in life and, ultimately, human suffering occurs because of sin. Saul dealt with a troubling spirit that caused him a form of mental illness. At times, suffering is indeed caused by demonic activity, while at other times, mental disorders are caused by biological, genetic, and physiological problems. In any case, the suffering is very real. Misdiagnosis and improper treatment of those suffering mental illness occurs when there is failure to understand the distinction between sin, mental illnesses, and demonic influence. Some cases require spiritual warfare; however, most of the time, the problem is not demonic. Christians must realize that physicians and medicines are necessary parts of the treatment of many mental illnesses.

In order for the church to deal properly with mental disorders, Christians must work together with the mental health professions. Christian psychiatrists and counselors should work closely with a patient's pastor, the one who maintains an ongoing relationship with the patient. The church is critical in caring for those with mental disorders. Those who suffer with mental disorders are in need of the unconditional love of Christians in order to find healing.

For more on **mental illness**, see the article by Paul Meier, Tim Clinton, and George Ohlschlager in **The Soul Care Bible**, page 364 (1 Sam. 16:14–23).

Mentoring

1 Kings 2:1, 2

Now the days of David drew near that he should die, and he charged Solomon his son, saying: "I go the way of all the earth; be strong, therefore, and prove yourself a man."

 When David handed over the kingdom of Israel to his son, we can be sure that he had prepared Solomon ahead of time. Solomon was given a huge responsibility, but his father had taught him many things about running the kingdom. When someone prepares another to take over his or her job or position, that is called "mentoring."

Jesus mentored his disciples, for they too would have a huge responsibility when He returned to heaven. He was a "master mentor." He gave us a good example to follow, for we should be mentoring new believers so that they can mature in Christ. A successful mentor:

- must be a good example to the people he or she is mentoring.

- must be able to share the Good News of Christ.

- must be committed to intercessory prayer.

- will care for and stand by those in need of help, whether it be through verbal encouragement, spending time with another, sharing a meal, providing help, or giving a hug.

- will study God's Word continually in order to teach others.

- has students who become mentors for others.

For more on **mentoring**, see the article by Don Hawkins in **The Soul Care Bible**, page 430 (1 Kin. 1—2).

Money

2 Kings 5:20

But Gehazi, the servant of Elisha the man of God, said, "Look, my master has spared Naaman this Syrian, while not receiving from his hands what he brought; but as the LORD lives, I will run after him and take something from him."

 Secular society tells us that our emotional security is linked with our financial security. Even in Elisha's day, this servant wasn't about to let money get away—and most of us would not either. However, for Christians, financial freedom comes from mastering our money instead of allowing it to master us.

We have to choose whether we will store up treasure on this earth or in heaven (Matt. 6:19-20). If we choose the latter, we must acknowledge God's ownership of everything we have; we merely manage the resources He gives us. Managing these resources involves practicing principles to help us master our money. Spending less than we earn, avoiding the use of debt, maintaining liquidity, and setting long-term goals are four major principles that should guide the decisions we make about our money. They will help us master our money.

While each of these principles is important, the real path to financial freedom and emotional well-being is learning to give of the resources we have. Giving acknowledges our dependence on God, and it breaks money's power over us. When this happens, our hearts are able to pursue the treasure that is in heaven.

For more on money, see the article by Ron Blue in **The Soul Care Bible**, page 480 (2 Kin. 5:20–27).

Motherhood

Luke 1:26, 27

Now in the sixth month the angel Gabriel was sent by God to a city of Galilee named Nazareth, to a virgin betrothed to a man whose name was Joseph, of the house of David. The virgin's name was Mary.

Our culture determines a woman's worth by how much she is paid. Mothering is not seen as a job or a skill. Mothers are constantly battling negative feelings that make them feel insignificant and worthless. It is hard for many mothers to value their investment in their children when the culture judges mothering as having no value.

Mothers must see their value from God's perspective. God esteems mothering. He chose a mother, a special young woman named Mary, to bring His beloved Son into this world—to nurture, teach, and care for Him. In His Word, God says that mothering has great rewards in that "her children rise up and call her blessed" and her husband will praise her (Prov. 31:28).

Mothers influence the development of their children. From birth to age three, a child's environment greatly affects his or her brain structure and ability to learn. Through a mother's love, a child will discover how to love others, learn, and adjust to his or her environment. Mothering also makes a difference in the life of the mother, who can take great joy and value in knowing that her investment in her children will give them security and independence.

For more on **motherhood**, see the article by Elisa Morgan and Carol Kuykendall in **The Soul Care Bible**, page 1312 (Luke 1:26, 27).

Obedience

2 John 6

This is love, that we walk according to His commandments. This is the commandment, that as you have heard from the beginning, you should walk in it.

 God requires His children to obey Him at any cost. Obedience to God means we must deny ourselves and depend solely on Him.

God sometimes requires us to be obedient in giving more than we are willing to or going somewhere that we do not want to go. We need to remember that our focus must not be on ourselves or on our circumstances, but on Christ. Abraham is a perfect example of selfless obedience. God commanded him to sacrifice his own son, yet Abraham was willing to obey. Abraham trusted God and His promises, and was therefore willing to obey at any cost. We must also trust God in order to obey Him.

When we are obedient, God will bless us. The greatest blessing is God's love (2 John 6). God promised Abraham that He would bless him and multiply his descendants because of his obedience (Gen. 22:16-17).

The blessings God gives us do not necessarily mean health and wealth; indeed it may mean the opposite. God's blessings are sure and eternal. When we walk in obedience, we will never stumble, for God walks with us.

For more on obedience, see the article by Dawson McAllister in **The Soul Care Bible**, page 1686 (2 John 6).

Occult

I Samuel 28:7

Then Saul said to his servants, "Find me a woman who is a medium, that I may go to her and inquire of her." And his servants said to him, "In fact, there is a woman who is a medium at En Dor."

The existence of Satan and demons is taught in several Old Testament books and by every New Testament writer. Satanic worship and witchcraft have been around for centuries. When King Saul desperately needed guidance, he sought out a medium. The Bible, however, clearly condemns occult worship and witchcraft (for example, Ex. 22:18; Lev. 19:26; 1 Sam. 15:23).

Today, young people are turning to Satan worship at rapid rates. Satanism is becoming a fad in developed countries, and the United States has the fastest growing and most highly organized body of Satanists in the world. The psychological packaging of occultism has made it more appealing today because the occult provides a person with an experience that transcends their spiritual emptiness. Experimenting with the occult can be like an addiction, however. Once someone becomes involved with occultism, it is hard to quit. Even dabbling in the occult can lead to hard-core satanic cult activity.

In satanic worship, which includes satanic circles, ritual dances, incantations to the devil, human and animal sacrifices, and drinking blood, demons or the devil himself are called upon in some manifestation of destructive power. Christians need to take this aspect of spiritual warfare seriously if they are to effectively minister to today's generation.

For more on the occult, see the article by Jerry Johnston in **The Soul Care Bible**, page 382 (1 Sam. 28:7).

Pain

2 Corinthians 12:9

And He said to me, "My grace is sufficient for you, for My strength is made perfect in weakness." Therefore most gladly I will rather boast in my infirmities, that the power of Christ may rest upon me.

 Pain is a reminder to every human being that we are under a curse because of the Fall. However, pain is a necessary part of life. Pain warns us of danger. Pain deepens our faith. The Holy Spirit comforts, nurtures, consoles, and protects us when we experience pain. Ultimately, pain brings us closer to becoming more like Christ.

From our perspective, however, pain is costly to treat, it constantly attacks the mind and spirit, and it robs people of spiritual vitality and motivation. Paul asked God to take away a pain that he felt was curbing his ministry. God chose instead to work through Paul's weakness.

Pain management involves acceptance of the pain and willingness to deal with it. Dozens of strategies are used to manage and control pain. Emotional, spiritual, and mental strategies include prayer, praise, humor, hobbies and group activities, or writing. Physical strategies include medications, surgery, nerve stimulation, relaxation, and massage therapy. People with chronic pain must learn how to pace their work, improve nutrition and exercise programs, and rest. Most of all, they must stay hopeful. God promises that His grace is sufficient and His strength is made perfect in weakness.

For more on pain, see the article by Siang-Yang Tan and George Ohlschlager in **The Soul Care Bible**, page 1534 (2 Cor. 12:9).

Parenting

Proverbs 22:6

Train up a child in the way he should go, and when he is old he will not depart from it.

The Bible tells parents to train their children in the way they should go. Parenting is no easy task, and no one receives a training manual before becoming a parent. Following are several important characteristics of godly parenting.

Nurture: Parents must nurture (feed) their children physically, spiritually, mentally, emotionally, and socially.

Protection: There needs to be a balance of protection without over-protection. Parents must protect their children physically from the dangers and violence of this world, and protect their minds from things such as agnosticism, prejudice, hatred, materialism, and superficiality.

Creativity: Parents need to learn to be creative in how they discipline, spend money, plan for the future, and teach God's Word to their children.

Motivation: Parents need to motivate their children to understand that they are part of God's plan and that their lives will make a difference for His Kingdom.

Relinquishment: The goal of parenting is to train up children to be godly adults. Releasing children into this world is scary, but parents must remember that their children are in God's care.

A Place for Returning: Children of godly parents will remember their parents with love and gratitude.

For more on parenting, see the article by Grace Ketterman in **The Soul Care Bible**, page 826 (Prov. 22:6).

Perfectionism

Hebrews 10:1

For the law, having a shadow of the good things to come, and not the very image of the things, can never with these same sacrifices, which they offer continually year by year, make those who approach perfect.

Perfectionists are people who believe they must be perfect in all they do. A definition of perfectionism should include both theological and psychological perspectives.

Theologically, perfectionism is the belief that one can be perfect and equal to God. When perfectionists do not know everything, they beat themselves up. When they think they should be all-powerful, they hate when things get out of control. When they think they should be able to do more than what is humanly possible, they get discouraged when they fall short.

Psychologically, perfectionists think about the way things *should* be instead of what is reality, set impossible goals, and believe that contentment can only come when they finish a project. They believe they must be the best at everything and equate their worth with their performance.

Perfectionists must learn to alter their expectations by humbling themselves before God and repenting of pride, facing reality, setting attainable goals and realistic time limits, and accepting being "good enough." They should discontinue black-and-white thinking, learn from their mistakes, and joyfully find their worth in God.

Perfectionists need to remember that they are already seen as perfect by God. He died to make them perfect before Him.

For more on **perfectionism**, see the article by Chris Thurman in **The Soul Care Bible**, page 1630 (Heb. 10:1).

Praise and Worship

Psalm 149:1

Praise the LORD! Sing to the LORD a new song, and His praise in the assembly of saints.

 We were created to worship God. Praising God puts us in line with our purpose and should be central to our lives. Praise is a special way that we can relate to our God. It si also a source of energy and power in our lives. Praise changes us as we focus on God and what He has done.

Our faith is both expressed and strengthened through praise. True praise does not seek to manipulate God but is the expression of our acceptance of our circumstances. It is when we trust God completely that He is free to bring victory in our lives. Praising God focuses our attention on His power.

Through praise we offer ourselves completely to God, both in times of joy and difficulty. Praising God in everything produces in us a peace that we may not have thought possible. God replaces our pain and confusion with peace, freedom, and joy. We are not commanded to *feel* thankful but to *be* thankful.

As we fulfill our purpose of praising God, our faith and relationship with Him are deepened. Through praise and worship, we experience the purpose, power, unity, and peace that only God can bring.

For more on praise and worship, see the article by Al Denson in **The Soul Care Bible**, page 794 (Ps. 149).

Prayer

Matthew 6:6, 7

"But you, when you pray, go into your room, and when you have shut your door, pray to your Father who is in the secret place; and your Father who sees in secret will reward you openly. And when you pray, do not use vain repetitions as the heathen do. For they think that they will be heard for their many words."

 We can enter into God's presence through prayer. It is the only way to find the peace, health, growth, fulfillment, and restoration that our souls so desperately need.

When we pray, we talk to God and share our hearts with Him. Jesus said that our prayers should not be full of "vain repetitions" or wordiness. Instead, we should communicate honestly with God and listen to His voice. Prayer allows us to get to know Him better and become more like Him.

The Bible tells us to "pray without ceasing" (1 Thess. 5:17). Prayer should be a way of life for us, infiltrating everything that we do. And when we ask for something, we should be specific. God will not always answer our prayers right away, but He will hear our prayers and answer in His time.

We can learn to make our prayers more effective and powerful. Effective prayer includes telling God that we love Him, praising Him for who He is, thanking Him for what He has done, declaring our dependence on Him, confessing our sin, sharing what is in our hearts, waiting on God to speak to our hearts, and thanking Him for listening.

For more on prayer, see the article by Stormie Omartian in **The Soul Care Bible**, page 1238 (Matt. 6:5–13).

Prejudice

James 2:8, 9

If you really fulfill the royal law according to the Scripture, "You shall love your neighbor as yourself," you do well; but if you show partiality, you commit sin, and are convicted by the law as transgressors.

 Prejudice occurs when people make premature judgments about others before objectively knowing all the facts. Prejudice involves negative attitudes, thoughts, and opinions toward others that often lead to discriminating behavior. Prejudice negatively affects the way people see themselves, as they wrongly separate themselves from others.

Ultimately, it also affects people's relationship with God, for prejudice draws them away from becoming like Christ. God does not show favoritism (Rom. 2:11). He desires that His children imitate His Son and learn to love others without showing partiality. God requires Christians to show love, kindness, and forgiveness to others. He also desires that they serve and edify others. James makes it clear that when we show partiality, we "commit sin."

Overcoming prejudice involves renewing the mind (Eph. 4:23). This is done through reading God's Word and learning to have the mind of Christ, who helps people develop impartiality, acceptance, unity, faith, love, peace, honor, hope, and humility (James 4:10). When Christians think of others, they must remember that everyone is fearfully and wonderfully made (Ps. 139:14). They must learn to see the beauty of God's creation in everyone.

For more on prejudice, see the article by Sabrina D. Black and Paris M. Finner-Williams in **The Soul Care Bible**, page 1646 (James 2:1–9).

Premarital Relationships

Ruth 3:10

Then he said, "Blessed are you of the LORD, my daughter! For you have shown more kindness at the end than at the beginning, in that you did not go after young men, whether poor or rich."

 For Ruth and Boaz, building a relationship was very different than today. In our culture, people "date," spending time getting to know each other. If two people fall in love, they may have a tendency to overlook potential problems. During this time of intense and deep emotion, the people dating are also trying to consider if this is the person with whom they want to spend the rest of their lives. Obviously, when people are playing the dating game, they should seek wisdom from God. He alone can help them to see clearly when love might otherwise blind them.

Marriage is a union not to be broken; therefore, people dating should take enough time to get to know each other. God's wisdom will help clarify the person's positive and negative characteristics. It is important to discover the other person's character: Is he/she a believer? Does he/she have a heart for God? Is he/she spiritual or worldly; humble or self-centered; genuine or deceptive?

Those who are dating must seek God's wisdom and guidance—and then be willing to follow it. The Lord will gladly provide you with wisdom as you search for a mate.

For more on premarital relationships, see the article by Les and Leslie Parrott in **The Soul Care Bible**, page 338 (Ruth 3:10–14).

Presence of the Holy Spirit

John 16:7

"Nevertheless I tell you the truth. It is to your advantage that I go away; for if I do not go away, the Helper will not come to you; but if I depart, I will send Him to you."

 Jesus promised His disciples that the Holy Spirit (here called "the Helper") would come to guide them in God's truth and help them through every difficulty. The Holy Spirit dwells in all believers, giving us strength to live for Christ (Eph. 5:18) and to bear the fruit of Christian character (Gal. 5:22, 23).

The Holy Spirit, along with the Father and the Son, makes up the Trinity. The Holy Spirit is unseen, but He is depicted in Scripture by certain symbols that help us understand His ministry. He is described as breath or wind (Ezek. 37:9), a dove (Luke 3:22), oil (Luke 4:18; Heb. 1:9), fire (Mark 9:49), a seal (Eph. 1:13; 4:30), and a guarantee (Eph. 1:14; 2 Cor. 1:22).

The Holy Spirit ministered to Jesus throughout His earthly life. Jesus was also anointed, filled with, led by, and raised to life through the Holy Spirit. Likewise, the Holy Spirit ministers to all Christians. He calls us to Christ, allowing us to experience God's grace. He also gives us assurance in our relationship with God. God speaks to us by His Holy Spirit. With the Holy Spirit in our lives, God is always with us.

For more on **presence of the Holy Spirit**, see the article by Ed Hindson in **The Soul Care Bible**, page 1400 (John 16:5–15).

Pride

2 Chronicles 26:16

But when he was strong his heart was lifted up, to his destruction, for he transgressed against the LORD his God by entering the temple of the LORD to burn incense on the altar of incense.

 Confidence is healthy when we put our confidence in God. Personal pride, however, can be very destructive. Pride is at the center of our sinful nature. In Scripture we see examples where pride led to disastrous consequences. Pride motivated Adam and Eve to disobey God (Gen. 3:4-6). Pride caused Satan to rebel against God (Is. 14:13-14; Ezek. 28:11-19).

There are many pitfalls for proud people. Pride makes it difficult for people to admit their weaknesses and ask for help, even help from God. Proud people are often difficult to work with because they cannot allow input from others or give credit to others. Pride is a way of making some people feel better about themselves at the expense of others—causing them to often be boastful, arrogant, or rude.

Pride can be defeated by humility. Humility focuses people's attention on the needs of others and is exemplified by love. People can develop humility by having a healthy view of God and spending time in worship and in thanksgiving. These practices can help people to cope with pride and see themselves as they really are before God.

For more on pride, see the article by Stuart Briscoe in **The Soul Care Bible**, page 572 (2 Chr. 26:16–19).

Relationships

Ecclesiastes 4:9

Two are better than one, because they have a good reward for their labor.

 God created us for relationships. The Bible tells us that building good relationships is an important part of life. In order to be able to build positive relationships, we should have several qualities.

We need to be people who listen. Being a good listener is vital to any good relationship and requires taking the time to hear what the other is saying. We need to be "safe" people; in other words, people who create security in our relationships. We need to be willing to help or give reassurance. Positive relationships are built when we can walk in others' shoes. If we learn to see the world from others' perspectives, we can better understand them.

We also need to be people who can receive as well as give. Meeting each other's needs is part of a healthy relationship and requires both giving and receiving. If troubles come into a relationship, we need to be able to weather them. Difficulties in relationships are almost inevitable, but they can lead to a deeper, more genuine relationship. Some relationships will have an ending point and we need to be able to call it quits if needed.

Building good relationships takes work, but it is well worth it.

For more on relationships, see the article by Les and Leslie Parrott in **The Soul Care Bible**, page 856 (Eccl. 4:9).

Repentance

Psalm 51:17

The sacrifices of God are a broken spirit, a broken and a contrite heart—these, O God, You will not despise.

 After King David committed adultery with Bathsheba, God used Nathan the prophet to confront him (read the story in 2 Samuel 11-12). David acknowledged his sin and repented. As with David, repentance begins with recognition of sin. Recognition of sin can come from our conscience, through the words of another person, or through reading God's Word.

When we recognize our sin, we should respond with sorrow. Fortunately, however, God doesn't leave us there. He says that we can repent. Through repentance, we can be set free from the power of sin. Repentance strengthens our relationship with God and with others, brings healing, and sets people free. Repentance can only happen when we accept responsibility for our sin and confess it to God. God can use our own humility and brokenness to teach others the path of recognizing sin, repenting of sin, and accepting God's remedy for sin.

God wants us to bring our sin into the open through confession and repentance, for only then can we be cleansed and healed. We must have an attitude of openness so that when God reveals our sin to us, we will be quick to repent and be restored.

For more on repentance, see the article by E. Glenn Wagner in **The Soul Care Bible**, page 722 (Ps. 51).

Responsibility

Jeremiah 1:9, 10

Then the LORD put forth His hand and touched my mouth, and the LORD said to me: "Behold, I have put My words in your mouth. See, I have this day set you over the nations and over the kingdoms, to root out and to pull down, to destroy and to throw down, to build and to plant."

Fulfilling our responsibilities can be difficult. We can find ourselves looking for excuses rather than facing the chance of failure. When God calls us to a task, He will equip us to accomplish it. We only need to seek Him, and He will provide everything we need in order to fulfill the task He has called us to do.

God's calling of Jeremiah shows how He equips people for the work He calls them to do. God equips people with His *presence* (Jer. 1:8), which comforts and sustains. Throughout the fulfilling of our duty, God remains with us and provides strength in the face of obstacles. God equips people with His *Word* (Jer. 1:9). God's Word is powerful, and we need to read, study, meditate on, and apply it to help us meet our responsibilities. God also equips people with His *promises* (Jer. 1:10). God promised that He would accomplish great things through Jeremiah before he even set out. God's promises can strengthen us when we face great responsibilities.

Remembering that God equips us with His presence, His Word, and His promises will enable us to face all the responsibilities God gives us.

For more on responsibility, see the article by Woodrow Kroll and Don Hawkins in **The Soul Care Bible**, page 962 (Jer. 1:8–10).

Restoration

John 21:19

This He spoke, signifying by what death he would glorify God. And when He had spoken this, He said to him, "Follow Me."

 Relationships are broken because of sin. But relationships can be restored through repentance and forgiveness. After Peter betrayed Jesus three times, Jesus forgave him and restored him as a disciple with the words, "Follow me." David was also restored to the fellowship of God after he committed adultery because he repented of his sin.

Restoration comes to Christians when they confess their sin, repent of it, accept responsibility for the consequences, face the truth of their actions, allow God to give them humility, and live with joy in their renewed relationship.

God calls Christians to be involved in the restoration of others (Gal. 6:1-5), and He gives guidelines for them to follow. First of all, they must be gentle toward the sinner. They must also bear the other's burdens by being active in helping the person. Helping others must never lead to pride; Christians need to be humble in knowing they are God's instruments. In order for Christians to avoid the sin of pride, they must understand their own weaknesses while not ignoring their abilities. They need to follow the Holy Spirit's lead, as it is the Spirit who brings about restoration through the efforts of His people.

For more on restoration, see the article by Earl and Sandra Wilson in **The Soul Care Bible**, page 1412 (John 21:15–19).

Salvation

John 3:16

"For God so loved the world that He gave His only begotten Son, that whoever believes in Him should not perish but have everlasting life."

 In the Bible, "salvation" refers to deliverance from sin and its consequences of death and eternity in hell. God has given us His gift of salvation, as seen in John 3:16. He loved us so much that He sent His Son, Jesus Christ, to die in our place and atone for our sins.

Because everyone is sinful (Rom. 3:23), all need God's grace and forgiveness of sins. Jesus died so that we might live forever with God. He demonstrated God's love for us by taking the punishment of our sins so that we might be saved. Through Jesus' death we are given salvation, and through His resurrection we are guaranteed eternal life.

Salvation involves *justification* (being declared righteous by God) and *redemption* (being freed from the condemnation of death through the payment of Christ's blood for our sin). Salvation cannot be earned, and no one deserves it. It is a gift of God's grace to humanity. In order to receive salvation, we must receive it as a gift, through faith. God invites everyone to accept His gift of salvation. "For whoever calls on the name of the Lord shall be saved" (Rom. 10:13).

For more on salvation, see the article by James Clinton in **The Soul Care Bible**, page 1372 (John 3:16).

Self-Denial

Luke 14:33

"So likewise, whoever of you does not forsake all that he has cannot be My disciple."

 Being totally committed to God means that we ask Him to take control over our lives. In Luke 14, Jesus said that people who are not fully committed to Him cannot be His disciples.

Christians must love Jesus Christ more than our personal relationships. This means that our love for Jesus must transcend our love even for our families.

Christians must love Jesus Christ more than our personal lives. Our personal priorities cannot be more important to us than the lordship of Jesus over our entire lives. This includes our jobs, reputations, and accomplishments. We cannot love our personal rights more than Jesus. His lordship must extend over our rights, choices, decisions, goals, and plans. This involves our complete identification with Him despite persecution and regardless of what we think is fair or what we want.

Finally, Christians must love Jesus Christ more than our personal resources. Everything we own, achieve, share, and give is transcended by the lordship of Christ.

A complete commitment to Jesus Christ means that His lordship is more important to us than our relationships, lives, rights, and resources. What God gives in return is greater than all these.

For more on self-denial, see the article by Vernon Brewer in **The Soul Care Bible**, page 1346 (Luke 14:25–33).

Self-Esteem

Jeremiah 1:5

"Before I formed you in the womb I knew you; before you were born I sanctified you; I ordained you a prophet to the nations."

 Self-esteem refers to how we feel about ourselves and what we think we can become. Paul encourages us to "think soberly" when evaluating ourselves (Rom. 12:3). Because of sin, we are not always able to think honestly about ourselves. As a result, many of us have low self-esteem. We do not accept ourselves and carry around feelings of self-hate and rejection.

If we are experiencing low self-esteem, we can learn to become more honest about the way we view ourselves by following certain guidelines. We should stop degrading ourselves. God created us, so when we degrade ourselves, we are, in essence, criticizing Him. We must value the gifts that God has given us and praise Him for making us who He wants us to be. We need to learn to value ourselves, because our value comes from God. He gives us strengths and helps us work on our weaknesses. We also need to learn to value others. All of these will help to build our self-esteem.

Christians, of all people, should have high self-esteem. Just as God knew the prophet Jeremiah before he was born and marked his life for service to Him, God also has a plan for every believer.

For more on self-esteem, see the article by Archibald D. Hart in **The Soul Care Bible**, page 960 (Jer. 1:5).

Sex in Marriage

1 Corinthians 7:3, 4

Let the husband render to his wife the affection due her, and likewise also the wife to her husband. The wife does not have authority over her own body, but the husband does. And likewise the husband does not have authority over his own body, but the wife does.

 God designed man and woman to be united as one flesh (Gen. 2:24-25). People were created to share their bodies with their spouses, find pleasure in each other sexually, and honor God with their pleasure. Married couples can experience fulfillment in sex when they affirm the Bible's teaching about sex in marriage and adopt helpful sexual attitudes.

Sex in marriage is intended for unity and pleasure, as well as for procreation. The Bible endorses sexual pleasure. It teaches husbands and wives to delight in giving themselves to one another.

Husbands and wives must practice respect and responsibility toward one another in order to have mutual sexual fulfillment. Women need to feel loved by and connected with their husbands in order to open up sexually. Men, on the other hand, feel loved and connected through sex. When the husband selflessly loves and connects with his wife and the wife openly shares her sexuality with her husband, they can find mutual fulfillment.

Married couples can find sexual satisfaction when they plan times for pleasure and when they affirm God's design for sex.

For more on sex in marriage, see the article by Clifford L. Penner and Joyce J. Penner in **The Soul Care Bible**, page 1500 (1 Cor. 7:1–9).

Sexual Integrity

2 Timothy 2:22

Flee also youthful lusts; but pursue righteousness, faith, love, peace with those who call on the Lord out of a pure heart.

 Many people appear to be in pursuit of sexual purity without being completely obedient. They are disobedient by being involved in sexual activities outside of marriage—these activities may not include intercourse, but that doesn't mean they have sexual integrity. The Bible tells us to "flee youthful lusts" and live with pure hearts.

It costs to be obedient and maintain sexual integrity. It is difficult to control our eyes, hearts, and minds when faced with sexual temptations. God requires His children to stay sexually pure for our own good and for His kingdom. We must daily fight the spiritual battle for purity, no matter what the cost. So many Christians have fallen to sexual impurity because they are unwilling to work at obeying. They have ignored the sacrifice that Christ made when He obediently suffered and died for them.

Becoming truly obedient requires that we recognize areas in our lives where we tolerate sin. Then we must hold these to the standards God provides in His Word and learn to live more like Christ. When we have sexual integrity, God gives us hope and joy, and obedience causes our faith to grow.

For more on sexual integrity, see the article by Stephen Arterburn in **The Soul Care Bible**, page 1608 (2 Tim. 2:22).

Sexual Sin

I Thessalonians 4:4, 5

Each of you should know how to possess his own vessel in sanctification and honor, not in passion of lust, like the Gentiles who do not know God.

 God calls Christians to holiness and purity regarding their sexuality. Sexual messages are found everywhere we go, and we must learn to keep ourselves free from the temptations that surround us.

The Bible refers to many sexual sins. Lust is the desire to physically gratify sexual needs outside of marriage. Adultery and homosexuality are other forms of sexual sin. Common sexual perversions include exhibitionism, voyeurism, cross-dressing, and sexual abuse. People experiencing these types of perversion need professional help to deal with them. Pornography is another sexual sin, and it is thought to the foremost social problem today.

Sexual sin is usually the symptom of deeper issues such as loneliness, feelings of unimportance, trauma, or the seduction of the culture. In order to treat the sin, we must understand the causes.

Healing can take place for a sexual sinner. The person must admit, confess, and repent of the sin in order to find spiritual healing. Christian counselors or mentors may be needed to help keep the person accountable. The individual must take steps in self-control to flee temptation by avoiding places, people, or activities. Most importantly, he or she must seek the Holy Spirit's guidance to be renewed each day.

For more on sexual sin, see the article by Marnie C. Ferree and Mark R. Laaser in **The Soul Care Bible**, page 1582 (I Thess. 4:5).

Sexuality

Genesis 1:27

So God created man in His own image; in the image of God He created him; male and female He created them.

God created people for relationships—with Himself and with one another. He also created us with gender—male and female. Neither gender is more important than the other, for both were created in God's image. It is important to understand that God created sexuality. The Bible's concept of sexuality pictures the complexity of God Himself. His creation of opposite genders and sex itself provide the foundation for marriage and family. Understanding our sexuality is foundational to understanding who we are and knowing how to relate to God and to one another.

Unfortunately, sexuality and the sexual experience have been distorted by sin. Sex is sold through magazine covers and at the movies. It is seen as nothing more than selfish pleasure to be engaged in whenever one desires with whomever is convenient. Clearly this was not God's plan. He created sexual intimacy for the marriage relationship alone, and within those boundaries. To venture outside the boundaries—with premarital, extra-marital, or homosexual sex—is to invite pain and heartache. People need to create healthy sexual boundaries for their thought lives and their physical expressions of their sexuality. God would have us be pure in all of our relationships.

To read more on sexuality, see the article by Doug Rosenau in **The Soul Care Bible**, page 6 (Gen. 1:27, 28).

Sin

I Kings 8:35, 36

"When the heavens are shut up and there is no rain because they have sinned against You, when they pray toward this place and confess Your name, and turn from their sin because You afflict them, then hear in heaven, and forgive the sin of Your servants...."

 In order to deal with sin, we must first believe and confess Christ as Savior. Then the Holy Spirit indwells us and provides us with the power to overcome sin daily. Yet sin will challenge us for as long as we live. Christians can overcome sinful habits by training for godliness in the following areas:

The Mind: People who desire to overcome sin must make sure that God's Word is richly dwelling in their minds.

The Will: Christians must put off old sinful behaviors and replace them with godly behavior such as prayer, Bible study, and worship.

The Body: God intends for Christians to deal with their God-given physical desires according to guidelines provided in His Word.

The Emotions: Emotions show us whether or not someone's beliefs and behavior are supported by the truth, so Christians must pay careful attention to their emotions.

The Holy Spirit: Those who desire to experience God's peace and power must choose to be constantly filled with the Holy Spirit.

Community: Christians must surround themselves with other believers in order to grow to maturity in Christ.

For more on sin, see the article by Ron Hawkins in **The Soul Care Bible**, page 446 (I Kin. 8:31–40).

Singleness

Matthew 19:12

"For there are eunuchs who were born thus from their mother's womb, and there are eunuchs who were made eunuchs by men, and there are eunuchs who have made themselves eunuchs for the kingdom of heaven's sake. He who is able to accept it, let him accept it."

Single people are important in God's kingdom. Jesus noted that some people are single "for the kingdom of heaven's sake." Christian single people should find their identity in Christ, not in their marital status. Single people are whole and complete as individuals in their relationship with Christ.

Being single is as honorable as being married. Single people must come to terms with the fact that not everyone marries. Paul claimed that it is good for people to remain single as he was (1 Cor. 7:8). Those who know single people should empower them to live full lives as they seek God's direction. Part of seeking God's direction is learning to be content.

Instead of choosing loneliness, single people should surround themselves with trustworthy friends with whom they can have fun. They should hold each other accountable to make healthy, wise choices in all areas of life, including the area of celibacy. They should also seek to actively minister to others.

Honoring God while living single will place God at the center of one's life. As every area of life is brought under submission to God, He helps people handle their fears, desires, hopes, and dreams.

For more on singleness, see the article by Alan Corry in **The Soul Care Bible**, page 1262 (Matt. 19:12).

Spiritual Disciplines

Acts 2:46, 47

So continuing daily with one accord in the temple, and breaking bread from house to house, they ate their food with gladness and simplicity of heart, praising God and having favor with all the people. And the Lord added to the church daily those who were being saved.

 Spiritual disciplines are what believers do in order to draw close to God. Jesus commanded His disciples to love God and others, deny themselves, and trust His Word. We must also learn to follow these commandments.

Christian discipleship is serious business. We cannot be Christ's disciples if we do not give Jesus control over our relationships, rights, and riches (Luke 14:25-33). Jesus said to "seek first the kingdom of God and His righteousness" (Matt. 6:33). Christians must learn to cast aside selfishness and put God first.

The Bible mentions the spiritual disciplines of *prayer* (Mark 1:35), *fasting* (Acts 13:3), *meditation* (Ps. 1:2) and *study* (Phil. 4:8). These disciplines are our responses to God's work in our hearts. They must be learned and practiced. They help us focus on the things of God so we can worship Him. In addition, *worship* is the highest expression of our souls and draws us into God's presence. God desires for us to worship Him and love Him with all our heart, soul, mind, and strength. When we worship Him, we will be ready to serve Him.

The early church practiced these disciplines, and it grew and thrived. So can we.

For more on spiritual disciplines, see the article by Ed Hindson in **The Soul Care Bible**, page 1420 (Acts 2:46, 47).

Spiritual Growth

2 Peter 1:5–7

But also for this very reason, giving all diligence, add to your faith virtue, to virtue knowledge, to knowledge self-control, to self-control perseverance, to perseverance godliness, to godliness brotherly kindness, and to brotherly kindness love.

Spiritual growth is the process by which the traits of Christ are gradually developed in a Christian. Some people fail to understand their role in this process. Thinking that spiritual growth is their own endeavor leans too heavily on human willpower. Legalism, judgmentalism, fatigue, and defeat are results of this thinking. The opposite approach is misguided also. Not doing anything to spur on growth can lead to passivity. Spiritual growth cannot be controlled any more than a farmer controls the growth of his seed. It is a gift from God, yet we still have a role to play, just as the farmer does in the planting process.

Spiritual disciplines, relationships, pain and suffering, and cross-cultural experiences all help Christians to grow spiritually. Spiritual disciplines such as solitude, the study and meditation of Scripture, prayer, worship, service, and giving should be practiced by Christians who are interested in spiritual growth. Gathering corporately for worship and learning remind us of the importance of continued growth. Relationships where we can share our struggles and have accountability are also important for growth. Going through pain and suffering brings about growth (James 1:2–3).

Remember, as we grow in Christ, we are being prepared to live with Him forever!

For more on spiritual growth, see the article by John Ortberg in **The Soul Care Bible**, page 1670 (2 Pet. 1:5–11).

Spiritual Warfare

Ephesians 6:12

For we do not wrestle against flesh and blood, but against principalities, against powers, against the rulers of the darkness of this age, against spiritual hosts of wickedness in the heavenly places.

All Christians face spiritual warfare. We know that God is victorious, but we must be alert and courageous, because Satan fights back. The Bible teaches us to fight the enemy with truth, faith, repentance, prayer, love, and obedience.

In order to fight victoriously, we must put on the armor of God and His power. God is the armor. He is the attacker and invader in the spiritual war. We can fight darkness with the light of the message of Jesus Christ.

The Bible does not mention exorcism of demons in the context of spiritual warfare. There are five reasons why demon deliverance is a not a biblical understanding of spiritual warfare: First, it portrays our warfare as defensive, instead of offensive. Second, the struggles of spiritual warfare such as sin, unbelief, and confusion, are never cast out in biblical context. Third, Jesus and the apostles used truth, faith, repentance, and prayer to deal with sin, occult practices, temptation, and moral bondage. Fourth, people in the Bible who came out of an occult background did not come out of it through exorcism. Finally, because the devil works to destroy human hearts, God deals with evil through the repentance of sin.

For more on spiritual warfare, see the article by David Powlison in **The Soul Care Bible**, page 1560 (Eph. 6:10–20).

Stress

2 Samuel 22:7

"In my distress I called upon the LORD, and cried out to my God; He heard my voice from His temple, and my cry entered His ears."

 David had his share of stress! Enemies on every side, battles to be fought, a kingdom to build. In this chapter we read a song of praise David sang to the Lord, who rescued him from deep distress.

Because stress in our culture is inevitable, we must learn to manage it. God's Word has much to say about handling stress. We should seek to understand what God is doing in our situation, and then learn to be joyful in spite of the difficulty (James 1:2-4). When we are stressed, we may feel like we have no time to pray, but that is when we must! Prayer helps us to see God's perspective (Ps. 46:10). We also must guard our hearts and minds against negativity. We do not always understand God, but we can trust in His faithfulness and goodness (Prov. 4:12). We must choose our priorities and be intentional about the way we spend our time and energy (Ps. 90:12). If we need to cut back, say no, or slow down, then we must know our limits and be willing to abide by them (Ps. 103:14). Finally, in stressful times, we must cultivate a thankful heart by counting our blessings every day (1 Thess. 5:18).

For more on stress, see the article by Leslie Vernick in **The Soul Care Bible**, page 422 (2 Sam. 22).

Suffering

Job 9:28

"I am afraid of all my sufferings; I know that You will not hold me innocent."

Suffering is an inescapable part of life. Suffering may come as the result of personal sin and failure; it may come from another's sin; it may occur due to forces beyond our control (such as natural disasters). Being Christians does not exempt us from suffering. The story of Job in the Bible exemplifies this. Though at first Job wanted relief, eventually his suffering awoke deeper desires. He found that what he wanted was God's presence in his suffering.

Suffering is not exclusive to human beings. All of creation suffers, both animate and inanimate, due to inevitable death and decay. The entire creation eagerly awaits the time when it will finally be redeemed.

Suffering is also experienced by God. God grieves when His children suffer. Jesus suffered so that humans would not have to face eternal suffering.

Though painful, suffering can be helpful. It shows us what our hearts worship. Do we long for deliverance or for the Deliverer? Suffering purifies our hearts and deepens our desire for heaven. Our own suffering causes us to understand the suffering of others and helps us to know what we can do to help. God uses our suffering for our good and for His glory.

For more on **suffering**, see the article by Dan Allender in **The Soul Care Bible**, page 646 (Job 9:28).

Suicide

Judges 16:30

Then Samson said, "Let me die with the Philistines!" And he pushed with all his might, and the temple fell on the lords and all the people who were in it. So the dead that he killed at his death were more than he had killed in his life.

Samson had great potential, but unfortunately he caused himself plenty of problems! In the end, he committed suicide. While suicide may seem to be a way to solve one's problems permanently, as believers we know that is untrue. Suicide is really a selfish action; it focuses only on oneself and one's own pain. In trying to get rid of that pain, the person causes pain, guilt, and hurt to those around him or her.

People contemplating suicide may not actually desire to die. They may just not want to go on living in their present state, but they cannot see beyond it. They have no hope. If they have no coping skills, friends, professional help, or loved ones, their pain becomes unbearable.

Too often, Christians do not respond to those who need their support. Perhaps we are too busy, or we overlook people who are quietly suffering. Mature believers need to be sensitive to those around them so that they can sense a desperate need and be able to offer help. The church should be a safe place where people who are hurting to the point of hopelessness can find hope, peace, and love. No one is beyond God's healing touch.

For more on suicide, see the article by Gary P. Stewart in **The Soul Care Bible**, page 322 (Judg. 16:28–30).

Temptation

Genesis 39:7

And it came to pass after these things that his master's wife cast longing eyes on Joseph, and she said, "Lie with me."

Joseph was faced with a difficult temptation. Day after day his master's wife continued to throw herself at him. Joseph's strength in refusing the temptation is an example to us that, no matter how difficult, temptation *can* be resisted.

That said, temptation is sneaky. Satan knows when and how to tempt us. He knows where we are most vulnerable. He offers compelling reasons to compromise, to set aside our standards, to find the shades of gray in situations that should be black and white. Temptation comes when we are weak; it comes when we feel strong. In short, we are always targets for temptation because Satan always seeks to trip us up along the path of our Christian walk.

Temptation itself is not a sin, for Jesus was tempted. Yielding to temptation, however, *is* sinful. But we are never alone in our temptations. God promises to never allow us to be tempted beyond what he knows we can handle, and he also promises to always provide a way out (1 Corinthians 10:13). As we face a temptation, we can ask God to give us the strength to resist *and* to show us the escape route.

To read more on temptation, see the article by Gary and Barbara Rosberg in **The Soul Care Bible**, page 62 (Gen. 39:6–15).

Tolerance

Jude 4

For certain men have crept in unnoticed, who long ago were marked out for this condemnation, ungodly men, who turn the grace of our God into lewdness and deny the only Lord God and our Lord Jesus Christ.

Tolerance used to be defined as a recognition and respect of others' beliefs without necessarily agreeing with them. Yet our society has twisted the meaning of tolerance and defined it by saying that all beliefs are equal and that everyone should praise and endorse all beliefs. This new tolerance is a dangerous way of thinking, because any unpopular message is labeled "intolerant" and is repressed.

Christianity, because it claims to be the "only way," is a target of intolerance. As we share our faith, we may face unpopularity and even persecution. We will be tempted to keep silent about our faith. But we must not keep silent, for the sake of our families, the church, and the spreading of the gospel.

Christians must counter these new doctrines of tolerance by pursuing truth and practicing love. We must teach our children to embrace all people, but not all beliefs. Our children must learn to show respect for people without necessarily agreeing with them. We must humbly speak the truth, even if we become the object of hatred. We must love others even when their behavior offends us. And we must tell others the truth because we are concerned for their salvation.

For more on **tolerance**, see the article by Josh McDowell in **The Soul Care Bible**, page 1694 (Jude 3, 4).

Trauma

Psalm 18:4, 5

The pangs of death surrounded me, and the floods of ungodliness made me afraid. The sorrows of Sheol surrounded me; the snares of death confronted me.

 David faced deep trauma—to the point where he felt that death itself stared him in the face. Everyone faces suffering and problems, but some events in life cause pain that is deep and long-lasting. Counselors say that this is "trauma." People can go through life not realizing that some of their fears, worries, or reactions are a direct result of a trauma they experienced.

Invasion trauma occurs when something happens to a person that causes damage. *Abandonment trauma* occurs when something does *not* happen to a person. Trauma left unhealed can produce a variety of symptoms in different people, such as anxiety, panic disorders, depression, or additions. However, there is hope for recovery. Trauma survivors need to be educated about the nature of the trauma and confront any denial of the trauma. They need comforting and non-judgmental listeners who will offer hope. They should be able to express their anger about their trauma, which can be accomplished in a variety of ways. They need to grieve their losses, set appropriate boundaries, know that they did not deserve the hurt they received, be able to see the strengths they have gained as a result, and eventually, to be able to forgive.

For more on trauma, see the article by Mark R. Laaser in **The Soul Care Bible** page 690 (Ps. 18:2–6, 25–30).

Trials

Psalm 34:18

The LORD is near to those who have a broken heart, and saves such as have a contrite spirit.

 No one goes through life without experiencing trials, whether they be physical, relational, or financial. A painful human trial is the feeling of rejection. People who have experienced rejection have difficulty trusting others, are hypersensitive to rejection, have fear of criticism and anger, try to rescue needy people, tolerate disrespect and abuse, and have difficulty trusting God and His Word.

Three principles can be followed to help heal the pain of rejection:

Principle 1: Cultivate Increasing Intimacy with God
We learn to know God, His love, and His eternal presence when we cultivate a spiritual environment that fosters a relationship with Him.

Principle 2: Cultivate Increasingly Balanced Relationships with Others
Jesus respected and interacted with people. We need to follow His example by not being afraid to speak the truth about our views and values, even if it means running the risk of being rejected.

Principle 3: Cultivate Increasingly Realistic Expectations of Ourselves, Others, and God
Because people are sinners and will disappoint us, we must depend on God's help to handle the hurt of rejection. He is the only source of healing. He promises to meet our needs.

For more on trials, see the article by Sandra D. Wilson in **The Soul Care Bible**, page 706 (Ps. 34:18).

Trust

Nahum 1:7

The LORD is good, a stronghold in the day of trouble; and He knows those who trust in Him.

 Healthy relationships require trust. Unfortunately, many relationships are torn apart when trust is lost. Trust can be lost due to physical, sexual, or emotional abuse, trauma, death, constant criticism, or the absence of love and attention. Some people who lose trust often seek to control others in order to avoid being hurt, or they may give up on relationships altogether. People who cannot trust people may also have difficulty trusting God.

It is possible for people who have experienced loss of trust to learn to trust again. There are steps people can take in order to regain trust. They will need to identify their patterns of distrust. They must be honest about their painful experience and repent of their own wrong behavior. They will need to find others to help them understand God's goodness and develop trust in Him (Nah. 1:7). Rebuilding trust takes caution. Those who have control problems should learn to be cautious, encouraging, open, and vulnerable in relationships. They also need to find people to understand, encourage, and speak the truth about God to them. Then they must personally commit to Bible study and prayer.

Trust can be rebuilt, for when we trust in God we will never be disappointed.

For more on trust, see the article by Patrick Springle in **The Soul Care Bible**, page 1180 (Nah. 1:7).

Truth

Zechariah 8:16, 17

"'These are the things you shall do: Speak each man the truth to his neighbor; give judgment in your gates for truth, justice, and peace; let none of you think evil in your heart against your neighbor; and do not love a false oath. For all these are things that I hate,' says the LORD."

The postmodern world asserts that truth is relative. Christians, however, can speak the truth to others and make true judgments (Zech. 8:16) because they believe in a standard of *absolute truth*. God is absolute truth; He is the foundation for all truth (Deut. 32:4; John 14:6).

The Holy Spirit will lead us to the truth of God's Word so we can know, be, and do the truth. Being people of truth means being authentic and genuine. We must be honest with ourselves and with others in every part of our being. Truth inspires us to live authentically with others—in our speech, with our spouses, with our children, and with the anticipation of God's kingdom.

We must be truthful in order to help others understand grace (Eph. 2:8-9). They need to know they are of value and worth (Eph. 1:4-5). They must accept their limitations and failures, knowing that God can use painful experiences to help them grow. In truth, they can have joy and freedom (Gal. 5:1).

When we know the truth in Jesus Christ, we experience freedom from Satan's blinding deceptions and sin. With truth, we can have an intimate relationship with God (Ps. 145:18).

For more on truth, see the article by Freda V. Crews in **The Soul Care Bible**, page 1208 (Zech. 8:16, 17).

Values

Galatians 5:22, 23

But the fruit of the Spirit is love, joy, peace, longsuffering, kindness, goodness, faithfulness, gentleness, self-control.

 Moral relativism reigns in today's society. The Bible, however, teaches values that are eternal and always applicable. These values glorify God. God desires His children to rely on His standard about what is good, true, and morally pure, and then apply that standard to their lives.

Virtuous character happens through the freedom Christians have in Christ. We are dead to sin and free to walk in the Spirit (Gal. 5:16, 25). Walking in the Spirit means that we manifest the fruit of the Spirit in our daily lives. God's values are the fruit of the Spirit: love, joy, peace, longsuffering, kindness, goodness, faithfulness, gentleness, and self-control. Virtue comes when we decide to walk in the Spirit rather than in the flesh.

Virtue is strengthened through trials and pressures. Paul tells us that "tribulation produces perseverance; and perseverance, character" (Rom. 5:3-4). We gain maturity, temperance, and character as a result of difficulties.

As we live according to God's standards, we will experience peace and security. Although our circumstances will change, our values will not. And God will use our example to draw others to Himself.

For more on values, see the article by Craig and Janet Parshall in **The Soul Care Bible**, page 1544 (Gal. 5:22).

Violence

1 Chronicles 11:23

And he killed an Egyptian, a man of great height, five cubits tall. In the Egyptian's hand there was a spear like a weaver's beam; and he went down to him with a staff, wrested the spear out of the Egyptian's hand, and killed him with his own spear.

 Violence has occurred since the day that Cain killed Abel—and there is much violence in Scripture. Violence is evil, and God cares deeply for its victims. Christians are not immune to the effects of violence or to the use of it. So in a culture filled with violence, what can we do?

We are wise to protect ourselves from violent people, and we should do everything possible to remove ourselves from violent situations. We should expose violence, for when we speak up, someone else may be kept from harm. Some relationships call for Christians to speak the truth from a loving heart to the one who has committed the violence, hoping that he or she will value the relationship enough to change.

Christians should never be afraid to allow violent people to experience the consequences of their actions. It is not wrong to use legal means of protection. Finally, Christians can be gracious. When we do so, we show that the sin committed against us holds no power over us. It doesn't shape us or cause us to become evil. God can use our kindness to shame one who has hurt us, and perhaps to make a difference in that person's life.

For more on violence, see the article by Leslie Vernick in **The Soul Care Bible**, page 526 (1 Chr. 11:23).

Weakness

1 Corinthians 2:3, 4

I was with you in weakness, in fear, and in much trembling. And my speech and my preaching were not with persuasive words of human wisdom, but in demonstration of the Spirit and of power.

 Doubt, fear, and our natural human frailties—all of which are examples of our weaknesses—can cause some believers to think that those weaknesses disqualify them from serving God. They couldn't be more wrong! For when believers turn to God and admit their vulnerability, they can experience God's power in their weakness.

When we admit our weaknesses, people can identify with us, understanding that if God can work through us, then He can work through them. People who think that they must always look great, have it all together, and never make mistakes will quickly be exhausted, or they will be devastated should one of their weaknesses be revealed. Instead, when we allow God to work through our weaknesses, we understand that any success that occurs is His alone. He gets all the glory—and that's the whole point!

Paul showed us how to handle our weaknesses. When he preached in Corinth, he didn't depend on great oratory or persuasiveness. He came in weakness and allowed God to work through him. The people believed not because of Paul, but because of God working through Paul's weakness.

Are you weak? Let God go to work!

For more on weakness see the article by George Ohlschlager and Tim Clinton in **The Soul Care Bible**, page 1494 (1 Cor. 2:1–5).

Wisdom

1 Kings 3:11, 12

Then God said to him: "Because you ... have asked for yourself understanding to discern justice, behold, I have done according to your words; see, I have given you a wise and understanding heart, so that there has not been anyone like you before you, nor shall any like you arise after you."

Wisdom is a gift from God that enables us to live with spiritual clarity as we seek to know His will for our lives. Growing in God's wisdom will affect our daily choices and decisions.

King Solomon is recorded in the Bible as having asked God to give him wisdom in order to rule the nation well. So God gave him great wisdom—in fact, he is considered to be the wisest man who ever lived. Though he ruled his kingdom with profound wisdom, he failed to apply that same wisdom to his personal life, and his heart ended up far from God. From Solomon's example we can clearly see that wisdom must be practiced in every area of our lives.

Those who desire to have wisdom are promised it if they ask God (James 1:5). In Christ we can receive true wisdom, therefore, a relationship with Jesus Christ is essential to growing in godly wisdom. We will grow in the depth of our wisdom as we grow in Christ. As wisdom grows in us, it will guide our decisions and we will be better able to perceive the will of God in our lives.

For more on wisdom, see the article by Lloyd Ogilvie in **The Soul Care Bible**, page 436 (1 Kin. 3:5–14).

Women's Issues

Proverbs 31:30

Charm is deceitful and beauty is passing, but a woman who fears the LORD, she shall be praised.

 The woman of Proverbs 31 feared the Lord and is called "virtuous." Virtuous women in the Bible include Miriam, Ruth, Hannah, Esther, Mary the mother of Jesus, the prophetess Anna, Mary and Martha, Lydia, and Priscilla. In today's ever-shifting culture, women who desire to be virtuous must be grounded in the truths of Scripture and learn from the examples of the godly women of the Bible.

Despite what the world believes, charm and beauty are passing, but truly beautiful women fear the Lord. Such women make knowing God their top priority. They cultivate intimacy with God by reading His Word and listening to His Spirit. They are committed to knowing and living in the truth. They hold onto biblically based thinking. They seek healthy Christian relationships, and may desire to be a part of a Christ-centered support group to gain encouragement and accountability. They find or become a godly mentor and build that kind of relationship. They draw their sense of worth from God and not from their relationships.

The virtuous woman is not meant to call women to be perfect, but to cause them to seek spiritual maturity. Women must realize that only God can meet all their needs.

For more on women's issues, see the article by Sandra D. Wilson in **The Soul Care Bible**, page 846 (Prov. 31).

Work

2 Thessalonians 3:12

Now those who are such we command and exhort through our Lord Jesus Christ that they work in quietness and eat their own bread.

 In 2 Thessalonians 3:10-15, Paul encouraged the church to follow his own example of hard work. Some of the believers had stopped working as they waited for Christ's second coming. Paul stressed that those who did not work should not eat. Likewise, we must work to provide for the necessities of life.

Many people find themselves constantly searching for a better job, one where they will find fulfillment. Others become obsessed with their jobs and become workaholics. It is important to remember that God values work, and we must work for His glory. We must keep a proper balance between our work life and our relationship with God, our families, and our church.

God desires us to work purposefully to advance His kingdom. There are several things we can do to find a purposeful job. Career counseling is available to help us assess our interests and skills in order to find better employment. We can increase our understanding of our own abilities, increase our skills, determine how to attain new skills, and receive ongoing education. Above all, we must remember that work is a calling from God, and we must give Him the glory in all we do.

For more on work, see the article by Tim Clinton and George Ohlschlager in **The Soul Care Bible**, page 1590 (2 Thess. 3:10–15).

Worry

Luke 12:22

Then He said to His disciples, "Therefore I say to you, do not worry about your life, what you will eat; nor about the body, what you will put on."

 Jesus commanded us not to worry. Yet we all worry about finances, loved ones, jobs, health, and many other areas of life. Jesus desires for us to set our priorities in order and to "seek the kingdom of God" (Luke 12:31). If we want to seek God's Kingdom, we must pray, releasing our worries to God.

Along with prayer, we must also change. Worry is unproductive. We cannot change any situation through worrying. We can, however, affect the way we approach the situation by making changes in our lifestyle. Examples of changes we can make include getting facts to prevent unrealistic worry, setting deadlines to make decisions, praying daily about concerns, delegating responsibilities, getting proper nutrition, sleep, and exercise, organizing, and learning to say "no."

Freedom from worry comes when we find the balance of prayer and action in our lives. Jesus showed us the importance of prayer when He went to the desert to fast and pray. He also showed us the value of action when He healed, taught, and obeyed His Father. Above all, Jesus said that we don't need to worry because God knows everything and He will supply all of our needs.

For more on worry, see the article by Rosemarie Scotti Hughes in **The Soul Care Bible**, page 1340 (Luke 12:22–31).